# *DEAR BRUTUS*

*J.M. Barrie*

# Contents

# DEAR BRUTUS

BY

J.M. Barrie

## ACT I

The scene is a darkened room, which the curtain reveals so stealthily that if there was a mouse on the stage it is there still. Our object is to catch our two chief characters unawares; they are Darkness and Light. The room is so obscure as to be invisible, but at the back of the obscurity are French windows, through which is seen Lob's garden bathed in moon-shine. The Darkness and Light, which this room and garden represent, are very still, but we should feel that it is only the pause in which old enemies regard each other before they come to the grip. The moonshine stealing about among the flowers, to give them their last instructions, has left a smile upon them, but it is a smile with a menace in it for the dwellers in darkness. What we expect to see next is the moonshine slowly pushing the windows open, so that it may whisper to a confederate in the house, whose name is Lob. But though we may be sure that this was about to happen it does not happen; a stir among the dwellers in darkness prevents it.

These unsuspecting ones are in the dining-room, and as a communicating door opens we hear them at play. Several tenebrious shades appear in the lighted door-way and hesitate on the two steps that lead down into the unlit room. The fanciful among us may conceive a rustle at the same moment among the flowers. The engagement has begun, though not in the way we had intended.

VOICES.-- 'Go on, Coady: lead the way.' 'Oh dear, I don't see why I should go first.' 'The nicest always goes first.' 'It is a strange house if I am the nicest.' 'It is a strange house.' 'Don't close the door; I can't see where the switch is.' 'Over here.'

They have been groping their way forward, blissfully unaware of how they shall be groping there again more terribly before the night is out. Some one finds a switch, and the room is illumined, with the effect that the garden seems to have drawn back a step as if worsted in the first encounter. But it is only waiting.

The apparently inoffensive chamber thus suddenly revealed is, for a bachelor's home, creditably like a charming country house drawing-room and abounds in the little feminine touches that are so often best applied by the hand of man. There is nothing in the room inimical to the ladies, unless it be the cut flowers which are from the garden and possibly in collusion with it. The fireplace may also be a little dubious. It has been hacked out of a thick wall which may have been there when the other walls were not, and is presumably the cavern where Lob, when alone, sits chatting to himself among the blue smoke. He is as much at home by this fire as any gnome that may be hiding among its shadows; but he is less familiar with the rest of the room, and when he sees it, as for instance on his lonely way to bed, he often stares long and hard at it before chuckling uncomfortably.

There are five ladies, and one only of them is elderly, the Mrs. Coade whom a voice in the darkness has already proclaimed the nicest. She is the nicest, though the voice was no good judge. Coady, as she is familiarly called and as her husband also is called, each having for many years been able to answer for the other, is a rounded old lady with a beaming smile that has accompanied her from childhood. If she lives to be a hundred she will pretend to the census man that she is only ninety-nine. She has no other vice that has not been smoothed out of existence by her placid life, and she has but one complaint against the male Coady, the rather odd one that he has long forgotten his first wife. Our Mrs. Coady never knew the first one but it is she alone who sometimes looks at the portrait of her and preserves in their home certain mementoes of her, such as a lock of brown hair, which the equally gentle male Coady must have treasured once but has now forgotten. The first wife had been slightly lame, and in their brief married life he had carried so-licitously a rest for her foot, had got so accustomed to doing this, that after a quarter of a century with our Mrs. Coady he still finds footstools for her as if she were lame also. She has ceased to pucker her face over this, taking it as a kind little thoughtless attention, and indeed with the years has developed a friendly limp.

Of the other four ladies, all young and physically fair, two are married. Mrs. Dearth is tall, of smouldering eye and fierce desires, murky beasts lie in ambush in the labyrinths of her mind, she is a white-faced gypsy with a husky voice, most beautiful when she is sullen, and therefore frequently at her best. The other ladies when in conclave refer to her as The Dearth. Mrs. Purdie is a safer companion for the toddling kind of man. She is soft and pleading, and would seek what she wants by laying her head on the loved one's shoulder, while The Dearth might attain it with a pistol. A brighter spirit than either is Joanna Trout who, when her affections are not engaged, has a merry face and figure, but can dismiss them both at the important moment, which is at the word 'love.' Then Joanna quivers, her sense of humour ceases to beat and the dullest man may go ahead. There remains Lady Caroline Laney of the disdainful poise, lately from the enormously select school where they are taught to pronounce their r's as w's; nothing else seems to be taught, but for matrimonial success nothing else is necessary. Every woman who pronounces r as w will find a mate; it appeals to all that is chivalrous in man.

An old-fashioned gallantry induces us to accept from each of these ladies her own estimate of herself, and fortunately it is favourable in every case. This refers to their estimate of themselves up to the hour of ten on the evening on which we first meet them; the estimate may have changed temporarily by the time we part from them on the following morning. What their mirrors say to each of them is, A dear face, not classically perfect but abounding in that changing charm which is the best type of English womanhood; here is a woman who has seen and felt far more than her reticent nature readily betrays; she sometimes smiles, but behind that concession, controlling it in a manner hardly less than adorable, lurks the sigh called Knowledge; a strangely interesting face, mysterious; a line for her tombstone might be 'If I had been a man what adventures I could have had with her who lies here.'

Are these ladies then so very alike? They would all deny it, so we must take our own soundings. At this moment of their appearance in the drawing-room at least they are alike in having a common interest. No sooner has the dining-room door closed than purpose leaps to their eyes; oddly enough, the men having been got rid of, the drama begins.

ALICE DEARTH (the darkest spirit but the bravest). We must not waste a second. Our minds are made up, I think?

JOANNA. Now is the time.

MRS. COADE (at once delighted and appalled). Yes, now if at all; but should we?

ALICE. Certainly; and before the men come in.

MABEL PURDIE. You don't think we should wait for the men? They are as much in it as we are.

LADY CAROLINE (unlucky, as her opening remark is without a single r). Lob would be with them. If the thing is to be done at all it should be done now.

MRS. COADE. IS it quite fair to Lob? After all, he is our host.

JOANNA. Of course it isn't fair to him, but let's do it, Coady.

MRS. COADE. Yes, let's do it!

MABEL. Mrs. Dearth *is* doing it.

ALICE (who is writing out a telegram). Of course I am. The men are not coming, are they?

JOANNA (reconnoitring). NO; your husband is having another glass of port.

ALICE. I am sure he is. One of you ring, please.

(The bold Joanna rings.)

MRS. COADE. Poor Matey!

LADY CAROLINE. He wichly desewves what he is about to get.

JOANNA. He is coming! Don't all stand huddled together like conspirators.

MRS. COADE. It is what we are!

(Swiftly they find seats, and are sunk thereon like ladies waiting languidly for their lords when the doomed butler appears. He is a man of brawn, who could cast any one of them forth for a wager; but we are about to connive at the triumph of mind over matter.)

ALICE (always at her best before "the bright face of danger"). Ah, Matey, I wish this telegram sent.

MATEY (a general favourite). Very good, ma'am. The village post office closed at eight, but if your message is important--

ALICE. It is; and you are so clever, Matey, I am sure that you can persuade them to oblige you.

MATEY (taking the telegram). I will see to it myself, ma'am; you can depend on its going.

(There comes a little gasp from COADY, which is the equivalent to dropping a stitch in needle-work.)

ALICE (who is THE DEARTH now). Thank you. Better read the telegram, Matey, to be sure that you can make it out. (MATEY reads it to himself, and he has never quite the same faith in woman again. THE DEARTH continues in a purring voice.) Read it aloud, Matey.

MATEY. Oh, ma'am!

ALICE (without the purr). Aloud.

(Thus encouraged he reads the fatal missive.)

MATEY. 'To Police Station, Great Cumney. Send officer first thing to-morrow morning to arrest Matey, butler, for theft of rings.'

ALICE. Yes, that is quite right.

MATEY. Ma'am! (But seeing that she has taken up a book, he turns to LADY CAROLINE.) My lady!

LADY CAROLINE (whose voice strikes colder than THE DEARTH'S). Should we not say how many wings?

ALICE. Yes, put in the number of rings, Matey.

(MATEY does not put in the number, but he produces three rings from unostentatious parts of his person and returns them without noticeable dignity to their various owners.)

MATEY (hopeful that the incident is now closed). May I tear up the telegram, ma'am?

ALICE. Certainly not.

LADY CAROLINE. I always said that this man was the culpwit. I am nevaw mistaken in faces, and I see bwoad awwows all over youws, Matey.

(He might reply that he sees w's all over hers, but it is no moment for repartee.)

MATEY. It is deeply regretted.

ALICE (darkly). I am sure it is.

JOANNA (who has seldom remained silent for so long). We may as well tell him now that it is not our rings we are worrying about. They have just been a means to an end, Matey.

(The stir among the ladies shows that they have arrived at the more interesting point.)

ALICE. Precisely. In other words that telegram is sent unless--

(MATEY'S head rises.)

JOANNA. Unless you can tell us instantly whet peculiarity it is that all we ladies have in common.

MABEL. Not only the ladies; all the guests in this house.

ALICE. We have been here a week, and we find that when Lob invited us he knew us all so little that we begin to wonder why he asked us. And now from words he has let drop we know that we were invited because of something he thinks we have in common.

MABEL. But he won't say what it is.

LADY CAROLINE (drawing back a little from JOANNA). One knows that no people could be more unlike.

JOANNA (thankfully). One does.

MRS. COADE. And we can't sleep at night, Matey, for wondering what this something is.

JOANNA (summing up). But we are sure you know, and it you don't tell us-- quod.

MATEY (with growing uneasiness). I don't know what you mean, ladies.

ALICE. Oh yes, you do.

MRS. COADE You must admit that your master is a very strange person.

MATEY (wriggling). He is a little odd, ma'am. That is why every one calls him Lob; not Mr. Lob.

JOANNA. He is so odd that it has got on my nerves that we have been invited here for some sort of horrid experiment. (MATEY shivers.) You look as if you thought so too!

MATEY. Oh no, miss, I--he--(The words he would keep back elude him). You shouldn't have come, ladies; you didn't ought to have come.

(For the moment he is sorrier for them than for himself.)

LADY CAROLINE. (Shouldn't have come). Now, my man, what do you mean by that?

MATEY. Nothing, my lady: I--I just mean, why did you come if you are the kind he thinks?

MABEL. The kind he thinks?

ALICE. What kind does he think? Now we are getting at it.

MATEY (guardedly). I haven't a notion, ma'am.

LADY CAROLINE (whose w's must henceforth be supplied by the judicious reader). Then it is not necessarily our virtue that makes Lob interested in us?

MATEY (thoughtlessly). No, my lady; oh no, my lady. (This makes an unfavourable impression.)

MRS. COADE. And yet, you know, he is rather lovable.

MATEY (carried away). He is, ma'am, He is the most lovable old devil--I beg pardon, ma'am.

JOANNA. You scarcely need to, for in a way it is true. I have seen him out there among his flowers, petting them, talking to them, coaxing them till they simply *had* to grow.

ALICE (making use perhaps of the wrong adjective). It is certainly a divine garden.

(They all look at the unblinking enemy.)

MRS. COADE (not more deceived than the others). How lovely it is in the moonlight. Roses, roses, all the way. (Dreamily.) It is like a hat I once had when I was young.

ALICE. Lob is such an amazing gardener that I believe he could even grow hats.

LADY CAROLINE (who will catch it for this). He is a wonderful gardener; but is that quite nice at his age? What *is* his age, man?

MATEY (shuffling). He won't tell, my lady. I think he is frightened that the police would step in if they knew how old he is. They do say in the village that they remember him seventy years ago, looking just as he does to-day.

ALICE. Absurd.

MATEY. Yes, ma'am; but there are his razors.

LADY CAROLINE. Razors?

MATEY. You won't know about razors, my lady, not being married--as yet--excuse me. But a married lady can tell a man's age by the number of his razors. (A little scared.) If you saw his razors--there is a little world of them, from patents of the present day back to implements so horrible, you can picture him with them in his hand scraping his way through the ages.

LADY CAROLINE. You amuse one to an extent. Was he ever married?

MATEY (too lightly). He has quite forgotten, my lady. (Reflecting.) How long ago is it since Merry England?

LADY CAROLINE. Why do you ask?

MABEL. In Queen Elizabeth's time, wasn't it?

MATEY. He says he is all that is left of Merry England: that little man.

MABEL (who has brothers). Lob? I think there is a famous cricketer called Lob.

MRS. COADE. Wasn't there a Lob in Shakespeare? No, of course I am thinking of Robin Goodfellow.

LADY CAROLINE. The names are so alike.

JOANNA. Robin Goodfellow was Puck.

MRS. COADE (with natural elation). That is what was in my head. Lob was another name for Puck.

JOANNA. Well, he is certainly rather like what Puck might have grown into if he had forgotten to die. And, by the way, I remember now he does call his flowers by the old Elizabethan names.

MATEY. He always calls the Nightingale Philomel, miss--if that is any help.

ALICE (who is not omniscient). None whatever. Tell me this, did he specially ask you all for Midsummer week?

(They assent.)

MATEY (who might more judiciously have remained silent). He would!

MRS. COADE. Now what do you mean?

MATEY. He always likes them to be here on Midsummer night, ma'am.

ALICE. Them? Whom?

MATEY. Them who have that in common.

MABEL. What can it be?

MATEY. I don't know.

LADY CAROLINE (suddenly introspective). I hope we are all nice women? We don't know each other very well. (Certain suspicions are reborn in various breasts.) Does anything startling happen at those times?

MATEY. I don't know.

JOANNA. Why, I believe this is Midsummer Eve!

MATEY. Yes, miss, it is. The villagers know it. They are all inside their houses, to-night--with the doors barred.

LADY CAROLINE. Because of--of him?

MATEY. He frightens them. There are stories.

ALICE. What alarms them? Tell us--or--(She brandishes the telegram.)

MATEY. I know nothing for certain, ma'am. I have never done it myself. He has wanted me to, but I wouldn't.

MABEL. Done what?

MATEY (with fine appeal). Oh. ma'am, don't ask me. Be merciful to me, ma'am. I am not bad naturally. It was just going into domestic service that did for me; the accident of being flung among bad companions. It's touch and go how the poor turn out in this world; all depends on your taking the right or the wrong turning.

MRS. COADE (the lenient). I daresay that is true.

MATEY (under this touch of sun). When I was young, ma'am, I was offered a clerkship in the city. If I had taken it there wouldn't be a more honest man alive to-day. I would give the world to be able to begin over again.

(He means every word of it, though the flowers would here, if they dared, burst into ironical applause.)

MRS. COADE. It is very sad, Mrs. Dearth.

ALICE. I am sorry for him; but still--

MATEY (his eyes turning to LADY CAROLINE). What do you say, my lady?

LADY CAROLINE (briefly). As you ask me, I should certainly say jail.

MATEY (desperately). If you will say no more about this, ma'am--I'll give you a tip that is worth it.

ALICE. Ah, now you are talking.

LADY CAROLINE. Don't listen to him.

MATEY (lowering). You are the one that is hardest on me.

LADY CAROLINE. Yes, I flatter myself I am.

MATEY (forgetting himself). You might take a wrong turning yourself, my lady.

LADY CAROLINE, I? How dare you, man.

(But the flowers rather like him for this; it is possibly what gave them a certain idea.)

JOANNA (near the keyhole of the dining-room door). The men are rising.

ALICE (hurriedly). Very well, Matey, we agree--if the 'tip' is good enough.

LADY CAROLINE. You will regret this.

MATEY. I think not, my lady. It's this: I wouldn't go out to-night if he asks you. Go into the garden, if you like. The garden is all right. (He really believes this.) I wouldn't go farther--not to-night.

MRS. COADE. But he never proposes to us to go farther. Why should he to-night?

MATEY. I don't know, ma'am, hut don't any of you go--(devilishly) except you, my lady; I should like you to go.

LADY CAROLINE. Fellow!

(They consider this odd warning.)

ALICE. Shall I? (They nod and she tears up the telegram.)

MATEY (with a gulp). Thank you, ma'am.

LADY CAROLINE. You should have sent that telegram off.

JOANNA. You are sure you have told us all you know, Matey?

MATEY. Yes, miss. (But at the door he is more generous.) Above all, ladies, I wouldn't go into the wood.

MABEL. The wood? Why, there is no wood within a dozen miles of here.

MATEY. NO, ma'am. But all the same I wouldn't go into it, ladies--not if I was you.

(With this cryptic warning he leaves them, and any discussion of it is prevented by the arrival of their host. LOB is very small, and probably no one has ever looked so old except some newborn child. To such as watch him narrowly, as the ladies now do for the first time, he has the effect of seeming to be hollow, an attenuated piece of piping insufficiently inflated; one feels that if he were to strike against a solid object he might rebound feebly from it, which would be less disconcerting if he did not obviously know this and carefully avoid the furniture; he is so light that the subject must not be mentioned in his presence, but it is possible that, were the ladies to combine, they could blow him out of a chair. He enters portentously, his hands behind his back, as if every bit of him, from his domed head to his little feet, were the physical expressions of the deep thoughts within him, then suddenly he whirls round to make his guests jump. This amuses him vastly, and he regains his gravity with difficulty. He addresses MRS. COADE.)

LOB. Standing, dear lady? Pray be seated.

(He finds a chair for her and pulls it away as she is about to sit, or kindly pretends to be about to do so, for he has had this quaint conceit every evening since she arrived.)

MRS. COADE (who loves children). You naughty!

LOB (eagerly). It is quite a flirtation, isn't it?

(He rolls on a chair, kicking out his legs in an ecstasy of satisfaction. But the ladies are not certain that he is the little innocent they have hitherto thought him. The advent of MR. COADE and MR. PURDIE presently adds to their misgivings. MR. COADE is old, a sweet pippin of a man with a gentle smile for all; he must have suffered much, you conclude incorrectly, to acquire that tolerant smile. Sometimes, as when he sees other people at work, a wistful look takes the place of the smile, and MR. COADE fidgets like one who would be elsewhere. Then there rises before his eyes the room called the study in his house, whose walls are lined with boxes marked A. B. C. to Z. and A2. B2. C2. to K2. These contain dusty notes for his great work on the Feudal System, the notes many years old, the work, strictly speaking. not yet begun. He still speaks at times of finishing it but never of beginning it. He knows that in more favourable circumstances, for instance if he had been a poor man instead of pleasantly well to do, he could have flung himself avidly into that noble undertaking; but he does not allow his secret sorrow to embitter him or darken the house. Quickly the vision passes, and he is again his bright self. Idleness, he says in his game way, has its recompenses. It is charming now to see how he at once crosses to his wife, solicitous for her comfort. He is bearing down on her with a footstool when MR. PURDIE comes from the dining-room. He is the most brilliant of our company, recently notable in debate at Oxford, where he was runner-up for the presidentship of the Union and only lost it because the other man was less brilliant. Since then he has gone to the bar on Monday, married on Tuesday and had a brief on Wednesday. Beneath his brilliance, and making charming company for himself, he is aware of intellectual powers beyond his years. As we are about to see, he has made one mistake in his life which he is bravely facing.)

ALICE. Is my husband still sampling the port, Mr. Purdie?

PURDIE (with a disarming smile for the absent DEARTH). Do you know, I believe he is. Do the ladies like our proposal, Coade?

COADE. I have not told them of it yet. The fact is, I am afraid that it might tire my wife too much. Do you feel equal to a little exertion to-night, Coady, or is your foot troubling you?

MRS. COADE (the kind creature). I have been resting it, Coady.

COADE (propping it on the footstool). There! Is that more comfortable? Presently, dear, if you are agreeable we are all going out for a walk.

MRS. COADE (quoting MATEY). The garden is all right.

PURDIE (with jocular solemnity). Ah, but it is not to be the garden. We are going farther afield. We have an adventure for to-night. Get thick shoes and a wrap, Mrs. Dearth; all of you.

LADY CAROLINE (with but languid interest). Where do you propose to take us?

PURDIE. To find a mysterious wood. (With the word 'wood' the ladies are blown upright. Their eyes turn to LOB, who, however, has never looked more innocent).

JOANNE. Are you being funny, Mr. Purdie? You know quite well that there are not any trees for miles around. You have said yourself that it is the one blot on the landscape.

COADE (almost as great a humorist as PURDIE). Ah, on ordinary occasions! But allow us to point out to you, Miss Joanna, that this is Midsummer Eve.

(LOB again comes sharply under female observation.)

PURDIE. Tell them what you told us, Lob.

LOB (with a pout for the credulous). It is all nonsense, of course; just foolish talk of the villagers. They say that on Midsummer Eve there is a strange wood in this part of the country.

ALICE (lowering). Where?

PURDIE. Ah, that is one of its most charming features. It is never twice in the same place apparently. It has been seen on different parts of the Downs and on More Common; once it was close to Radley village and another time about a mile from the sea. Oh, a sporting wood!

LADY CAROLINE. And Lob is anxious that we should all go and look for it?

COADE. Not he; Lob is the only sceptic in the house. Says it is all rubbish, and that we shall be sillies if we go. But we believe, eh, Purdie?

PURDIE (waggishly). Rather!

LOB (the artful). Just wasting the evening. Let us have a round game at cards here instead.

PURDIE (grandly), No, sir, I am going to find that wood.

JOANNA. What is the good of it when it is found?

PURDIE. We shall wander in it deliciously, listening to a new sort of bird called the Philomel.

(LOB is behaving in the most exemplary manner; making sweet little clucking sounds.)

JOANNA (doubtfully). Shall we keep together, Mr. Purdie?

PURDIE. No, we must hunt in pairs.

JOANNA. (converted). I think it would he rather fun. Come on, Coady, I'll lace your boots for you. I am sure your poor foot will carry you nicely.

ALICE. Miss Trout, wait a moment. Lob, has this wonderful wood any special properties?

LOB. Pooh! There's no wood.

LADY CAROLINE. You've never seen it?

LOB. Not I. I don't believe in it.

ALICE. Have any of the villagers ever been in it?

LOB (dreamily). So it's said; so it's said.

ALICE. What did they say were their experiences?

LOB. That isn't known. They never came back.

JOANNA (promptly resuming her seat). Never came back!

LOB. Absurd, of course. You see in the morning the wood was gone; and so they were gone, too. (He clucks again.)

JOANNA. I don't think I like this wood.

MRS. COADE. It certainly is Midsummer Eve.

COADE (remembering that women are not yet civilised). Of course if you ladies are against it we will drop the idea. It was only a bit of fun.

ALICE (with a malicious eye on LOB). Yes, better give it up--to please Lob.

PURDIE. Oh, all right, Lob. What about that round game of cards?

(The proposal meets with approval.)

LOB (bursting into tears). I wanted you to go. I had set my heart on your going. It is the thing I wanted, and it isn't good for me not to get the thing I want.

(He creeps under the table and threatens the hands that would draw him out.)

MRS. COADE. Good gracious, he has wanted it all the time. You wicked Lob!

ALICE. Now, you see there *is* something in it.

COADE. Nonsense, Mrs. Dearth, it was only a joke.

MABEL (melting). Don't cry, Lobby.

LOB. Nobody cares for me--nobody loves me. And I need to be loved.

(Several of them are on their knees to him.)

JOANNA. Yes, we do, we all love you. Nice, nice Lobby.

MABEL. Dear Lob, I am so fond of you.

JOANNA. Dry his eyes with my own handkerchief. (He holds up his eyes but is otherwise inconsolable.)

LADY CAROLINE. Don't pamper him.

LOB (furiously). I need to be pampered.

MRS. COADE. You funny little man. Let us go at once and look for his wood.

(All feel that thus alone can his tears be dried.)

JOANNA. Boots and cloaks, hats forward. Come on, Lady Caroline, just to show you are not afraid of Matey.

(There is a general exodus, and LOB left alone emerges from his temporary retirement. He ducks victoriously, but presently is on his knees again distressfully regarding some flowers that have fallen from their bowl.)

LOB. Poor bruised one, it was I who hurt you. Lob is so sorry. Lie there! (To another.) Pretty, pretty, let me see where you have a pain? You fell on your head; is this the place? Now I make it better. Oh, little rascal, you are not hurt at all; you just pretend. Oh dear, oh dear! Sweetheart, don't cry, you are now prettier than ever. You were too tall. Oh, how beautifully you smell now that you are small. (He replaces the wounded tenderly in their bowl.) rink, drink. Now, you are happy again. The little rascal smiles. All smile, please--nod heads--aha! aha! You love Lob--Lob loves you.

(JOANNA and MR. PURDIE stroll in by the window.)

JOANNA. What were you saying to them, Lob?

LOB. I was saying 'Two's company, three's none.'

(He departs with a final cluck.)

JOANNA. That man--he suspects!

(This is a very different JOANNA from the one who has so far flitted across our scene. It is also a different PURDIE. In company they seldom look at each other, though when the one does so the eyes of the other magnetically respond. We have seen them trivial, almost cynical, but now we are to greet them as they know they really are, the great strong-hearted man and his natural mate, in the grip of the master passion. For the moment LOB'S words have unnerved JOANNA and it is JOHN PURDIE's dear privilege to soothe her.)

PURDIE. No one minds Lob. My dear, oh my dear.

JOANNA (faltering). Yes, but he saw you kiss my hand. Jack, if Mabel were to suspect!

PURDIE (happily). There is nothing for her to suspect.

JOANNA (eagerly). No, there isn't, is there? (She is desirous ever to be without a flaw.) Jack, I am not doing anything wrong, am I?

PURDIE. You!

(With an adorable gesture she gives him one of her hands, and manlike he takes the other also.)

JOANNA. Mabel is your wife, Jack. I should so hate myself if I did anything that was disloyal to her.

PURDIE (pressing her hand to her eyes as if counting them, in the strange manner of lovers). Those eyes could never be disloyal--my lady of the nut-brown eyes. (He holds her from him, surveying her, and is scorched in the flame of her femininity.) Oh, the sveldtness of you. (Almost with reproach.) Joanna, why are you so sveldt!

(For his sake she would be less sveldt if she could, but she can't. She admits her failure with eyes grown still larger, and he envelops her so that he may not see her. Thus men seek safety.)

JOANNA (while out of sight). All I want is to help her and you.

PURDIE. I know--how well I know--my dear brave love.

JOANNA. I am very fond of Mabel, Jack. I should like to be the best friend she has in the world.

PURDIE. You are, dearest. No woman ever had a better friend.

JOANNA. And yet I don't think she really likes me. I wonder why?

PURDIE (who is the bigger brained of the two.) It is just that Mabel doesn't understand. Nothing could make me say a word against my wife

JOANNA (sternly). I wouldn't listen to you if you did.

PURDIE. I love you all the more, dear, for saying that. But Mabel is a cold nature and she doesn't understand.

JOANNA (thinking never of herself but only of him). She doesn't appreciate your finer qualities.

PURDIE (ruminating). That's it. But of course I am difficult. I always was a strange, strange creature. I often think, Joanna, that I am rather like a flower that has never had the sun to shine on it nor the rain to water it.

JOANNA. You break my heart.

PURDIE (with considerable enjoyment). I suppose there is no more lonely man than I walking the earth to-day.

JOANNA (beating her wings). It is so mournful.

PURDIE. It is the thought of you that sustains me, elevates me. You shine high above me like a star.

JOANNA. No, no. I wish I was wonderful, but I am not.

PURDIE. You have made me a better man, Joanna.

JOANNA. I am so proud to think that.

PURDIE. You have made me kinder to Mabel.

JOANNA. I am sure you are always kind to her.

PURDIE. Yes, I hope so. But I think now of special little ways of giving her pleasure. That never-to-be-forgotten day when we first met, you and I!

JOANNA (fluttering nearer to him.) That tragic, lovely day by the weir. Oh, Jack!

PURDIE. Do you know how in gratitude I spent the rest of that day?

JOANNA (crooning). Tell me.

PURDIE. I read to Mabel aloud for an hour. I did it out of kindness to her, because I had met you.

JOANNA. It was dear of you.

PURDIE. Do you remember that first time my arms--your waist--you are so fluid, Joanna. (Passionately.) Why are you so fluid?

JOANNA (downcast). I can't help it, Jack.

PURDIE. I gave her a ruby bracelet for that.

JOANNA. It is a gem. You have given that lucky woman many lovely things.

PURDIE. It is my invariable custom to go straight off and buy Mabel something whenever you have been sympathetic to me. Those new earrings of hers--they are in memory of the first day you called me Jack. Her Paquin gown--the one with the beads--was because you let me kiss you.

JOANNA. I didn't exactly let you.

PURDIE. No, but you have such a dear way of giving in.

JOANNA. Jack, she hasn't worn that gown of late.

PURDIE. No, nor the jewels. I think she has some sort of idea now that when I give her anything nice it means that you have been nice to me. She has rather a suspicious nature, Mabel; she never used to have it, but it seems to be growing on her. I wonder why, I wonder why?

(In this wonder which is shared by JOANNA their lips meet, and MABEL, who has been about to enter from the garden quietly retires.)

JOANNA. Was that any one in the garden?

PURDIE (returning from a quest). There is no one there now.

JOANNA. I am sure I heard some one. If it was Mabel! (With a perspicacity that comes of knowledge of her sex.) Jack, if she saw us she will think you were kissing me.

(These fears are confirmed by the rather odd bearing of MABEL, who now joins their select party.)

MABEL (apologetically). I am so sorry to interrupt you, Jack; but please wait a moment before you kiss her again. Excuse me, Joanna. (She quietly draws the curtains, thus shutting out the garden and any possible onlooker.) I did not want the others to see you; they might not understand how noble you are, Jack. You can go on now.

(Having thus passed the time of day with them she withdraws by the door, leaving JACK bewildered and JOANNA knowing all about it.)

JOANNA. How extraordinary! Of all the--! Oh, but how contemptible! (She sweeps to the door and calls to MABEL by name.)

MABEL (returning with promptitude). Did you call me, Joanna?

JOANNA (guardedly). I insist on an explanation. (With creditable hauteur.) What were you doing in the garden, Mabel?

MABEL (who has not been so quiet all day). I was looking for something I have lost.

PURDIE (hope springing eternal). Anything important?

MABEL. I used to fancy it, Jack. It is my husband's love. You don't happen to have picked it up, Joanna? If so and you don't set great store by it I should like it back--the pieces, I mean.

(MR. PURDIE is about lo reply to this, when JOANNA rather wisely fills the breach.)

JOANNA. Mabel, I--I will not be talked to in that way. To imply that I--that your husband--oh, shame!

PURDIE (finely). I must say, Mabel, that I am a little disappointed in you. I certainly understood that you had gone upstairs to put on your boots.

MABEL. Poor old Jack. (She muses.) A woman like that!

JOANNA (changing her comment in the moment of utterance), I forgive you Mabel, you will be sorry for this afterwards.

PURDIE (warningly, but still reluctant to think less well of his wife). Not a word against Joanna, Mabel. If you knew how nobly she has spoken of you.

JOANNA (imprudently). She does know. She has been listening.

(There is a moment's danger of the scene degenerating into something mid-Victorian. Fortunately a chivalrous man is present to lift it to a higher plane. JOHN PURDIE is one to whom subterfuge of any kind is abhorrent; if he has not spoken out before it is because of his reluctance to give MABEL pain. He speaks out now, and seldom probably has he proved himself more worthy.)

PURDIE. This is a man's business. I must be open with you now, Mabel: it is the manlier way. If you wish it I shall always be true to you in word and deed; it is your right. But I cannot pretend that Joanna is not the one woman in the world for me. If I had met her before you--it's Kismet, I suppose. (He swells.)

JOANNA (from a chair). Too late, too late.

MABEL (although the woman has seen him swell). I suppose you never knew what true love was till you met her, Jack?

PURDIE. You force me to say it. Joanna and I are as one person. We have not a thought at variance. We are one rather than two.

MABEL (looking at JOANNA). Yes, and that's the one! (With the cheapest sarcasm.) I am so sorry to have marred your lives.

PURDIE. If any blame there is, it is all mine; she is as spotless as the driven snow. The moment I mentioned love to her she told me to desist.

MABEL. Not she.

JOANNA. So you were listening! (The obtuseness of MABEL is very strange to her.) Mabel, don't you see how splendid he is!

MABEL. Not quite, Joanna.

(She goes away. She is really a better woman than this, but never capable of scaling that higher plane to which he has, as it were, offered her a hand.)

JOANNA. How lovely of you, Jack, to take it all upon yourself.

PURDIE (simply). It is the man's privilege.

JOANNA. Mabel has such a horrid way of seeming to put people in the wrong.

PURDIE. Have you noticed that? Poor Mabel, it is not an enviable quality.

JOANNA (despondently). I don't think I care to go out now. She has spoilt it all. She has taken the innocence out of it, Jack.

PURDIE (a rock). We must be brave and not mind her. Ah, Joanna, if we had met in time. If only I could begin again. To be battered for ever just because I once took the wrong turning, it isn't fair.

JOANNA (emerging from his arms). The wrong turning! Now, who was saying that a moment ago--about himself? Why, it was Matey.

(A footstep is heard.)

PURDIE (for the first time losing patience with his wife). Is that her coming back again? It's too bad.

(But the intruder is MRS. DEARTH, and he greets her with relief.)

Ah, it is you, Mrs. Dearth.

ALICE. Yes, it is; but thank you for telling me, Mr. Purdie. I don't intrude, do I?

JOANNA (descending to the lower plane, on which even goddesses snap). Why should you?

PURDIE. Rather not. We were--hoping it would be you. We want to start on the walk. I can't think what has become of the others. We have been looking for them everywhere. (He glances vaguely round the room, as if they might so far have escaped detection.)

ALICE (pleasantly). Well, do go on looking; under that flower-pot would be a good place. It is my husband I am in search of.

PURDIE (who likes her best when they are in different rooms). Shall I rout him out for you?

ALICE. How too unutterably kind of you, Mr. Purdie. I hate to trouble you, but it would be the sort of service one never forgets.

PURDIE. You know, I believe you are chaffing me.

ALICE. No, no, I am incapable of that.

PURDIE. I won't be a moment.

ALICE. Miss Trout and I will await your return with ill-concealed impatience.

(They await it across a table, the newcomer in a reverie and JOANNA watching her. Presently MRS. DEARTH looks up, and we may notice that she has an attractive screw of the mouth which denotes humour.)

Yes, I suppose you are right; I dare say I am.

JOANNA (puzzled). I didn't say anything.

ALICE. I thought I heard you say 'That hateful Dearth woman, coming butting in where she is not wanted.'

(Joanna draws up her sveldt figure, but a screw of one mouth often calls for a similar demonstration from another, and both ladies smile. They nearly become friends.)

JOANNA. You certainly have good ears.

ALICE (drawling). Yes, they have always been rather admired.

JOANNA (snapping). By the painters for whom you sat when you were an artist's model?

ALICE (measuring her). So that has leaked out, has it!

JOANNA (ashamed). I shouldn't have said that.

ALICE (their brief friendship over). Do you think I care whether you know or not?

JOANNA (making an effort to be good). I'm sure you don't. Still, it was cattish of me.

ALICE. It was.

JOANNA (in flame). I don't see it.

(MRS. DEARTH laughs and forgets her, and with the entrance of a man from the dining room JOANNA drifts elsewhere. Not so much a man, this newcomer, as the relic of what has been a good one; it is the most he would ever claim for himself. Sometimes, brandy in hand, he has visions of the WILL DEARTH he used to be, clear of eye. sees him but a field away, singing at his easel or, fishing-rod in hand, leaping a stile. Our WILL stares after the fellow for quite a long time, so long that the two melt into the one who finishes LOB's brandy. He is scarcely intoxicated as he appears before the lady of his choice, but he is shaky and has watery eyes.)

(ALICE has had a rather wild love for this man, or for that other one, and he for her, but somehow it has gone whistling down the wind. We may expect therefore to see them at their worst when in each other's company.)

DEARTH (who is not without a humorous outlook on his own degradation). I am uncommonly flattered, Alice, to hear that you have sent for me. It quite takes me aback.

ALICE (with cold distaste). It isn't your company I want, Will.

DEARTH. You know. I felt that Purdie must have delivered your message wrongly.

ALICE. I want you to come with us on this mysterious walk and keep an eye on Lob.

DEARTH. On poor little Lob? Oh, surely not.

ALICE. I can't make the man out. I want you to tell me something; when he invited us here, do you think it was you or me he specially wanted?

DEARTH. Oh, you. He made no bones about it; said there was something about you that made him want uncommonly to have you down here.

ALICE. Will, try to remember this: did he ask us for any particular time?

DEARTH. Yes, he was particular about its being Midsummer week.

ALICE. Ah! I thought so. Did he say what it was about me that made him want to have me here in Midsummer week?

DEARTH. No, but I presumed it must be your fascination, Alice.

ALICE. Just so. Well, I want you to come out with us to-night to watch him.

DEARTH. Crack-in-my-eye-Tommy, spy on my host! And such a harmless little chap, too. Excuse me, Alice. Besides I have an engagement.

ALICE. An engagement--with the port decanter, I presume.

DEARTH. A good guess, but wrong. The decanter is now but an empty shell. Still, how you know me! My engagement is with a quiet cigar in the garden.

ALICE. Your hand is so unsteady, you won't be able to light the match.

DEARTH. I shall just manage. (He triumphantly proves the exact truth of his statement.)

ALICE. A nice hand for an artist!

DEARTH. One would scarcely call me an artist now-a-days.

ALICE. Not so far as any work is concerned.

DEARTH. Not so far as having any more pretty dreams to paint is concerned. (Grinning at himself.) Wonder why I have become such a waster, Alice?

ALICE. I suppose it was always in you.

DEARTH (with perhaps a glimpse of the fishing-rod). I suppose so; and yet I was rather a good sort in the days when I went courting you.

ALICE. Yes, I thought so. Unlucky days for me, as it has turned out.

DEARTH (heartily). Yes, a bad job for you. (Puzzling unsteadily over himself.) I didn't know I was a wrong 'un at the time; thought quite well of myself, thought a vast deal more of you. Crack-in-my-eye-Tommy, how I used to leap out of bed at 6 A.M. all agog to be at my easel; blood ran through my veins in those days. And now I'm middle-aged and done for. Funny! Don't know how it has come about, nor what has made the music mute. (Mildly curious.) When did you begin to despise me, Alice?

ALICE. When I got to know you really, Will; a long time ago.

DEARTH (bleary of eye). Yes, I think that is true. It was a long time ago, and before I had begun to despise myself. It wasn't till I knew you had no opinion of me that I began to go down hill. You will grant that, won't you; and that I did try for a bit to fight on? If you had cared for me I wouldn't have come to this, surely?

ALICE. Well, I found I didn't care for you, and I wasn't hypocrite enough to pretend I did. That's blunt, but you used to admire my bluntness.

DEARTH. The bluntness of you, the adorable wildness of you, you untamed thing! There were never any shades in you; kiss or kill was your motto, Alice. I felt from the first moment I saw you that you would love me or knife me.

(Memories of their shooting star flare in both of them for as long as a sheet of paper might take to burn.)

ALICE. I didn't knife you.

DEARTH. No. I suppose that was where you made the mistake. It is hard on you, old lady. (Becoming watery.) I suppose it's too late to try to patch things up?

ALICE. Let's be honest; it is too late, Will. DEARTH (whose tears would smell of brandy). Perhaps if we had had children--Pity!

ALICE. A blessing I should think, seeing what sort of a father they would have had.

DEARTH (ever reasonable). I dare say you're right. Well, Alice, I know that somehow it's my fault. I'm sorry for you.

ALICE. I'm sorry for myself. If I hadn't married you what a different woman I should be. What a fool I was.

DEARTH. Ah! Three things they say come not back to men nor women--the spoken word, the past life and the neglected opportunity. Wonder if we should make any more of them, Alice, if they did come back to us.

ALICE. You wouldn't.

DEARTH (avoiding a hiccup). I guess you're right.

ALICE. But I--

DEARTH (sincerely). Yes, what a boon for you. But I hope it's not Freddy Finch-Fallowe you would put in my place; I know he is following you about again. (He is far from threatening her, he has too beery an opinion of himself for that.)

ALICE. He followed me about, as you put it, before I knew you. I don't know why I quarrelled with him.

DEARTH. Your heart told you that he was no good, Alice.

ALICE. My heart told me that you were. So it wasn't of much service to me, my heart!

DEARTH. The Honourable Freddy Finch-Fallowe is a rotter.

ALICE (ever inflammable). You are certainly an authority on the subject.

DEARTH (with the sad smile of the disillusioned). You have me there. After which brief, but pleasant, little connubial chat, he pursued his dishonoured way into the garden.

(He is however prevented doing so for the moment by the return of the others. They are all still in their dinner clothes though wearing wraps. They crowd in through the door, chattering.)

LOB. Here they are. Are you ready, dear lady?

MRS. COADE (seeing that DEARTH's hand is on the window curtains). Are you not coming with us to find the wood, Mr. Dearth.

DEARTH. Alas, I am unavoidably detained. You will find me in the garden when you come back.

JOANNA (whose sense of humour has been restored). If we ever do come back!

DEARTH. Precisely. (With a groggy bow.) Should we never meet again, Alice, fare thee well. Purdie, if you find the tree of knowledge in the wood bring me back an apple.

PURDIE. I promise.

LOB. Come quickly. Matey mustn't see me. (He is turning out the lights.)

LADY CAROLINE (pouncing). Matey? What difference would that make, Lob?

LOB. He would take me off to bed; it's past my time.

COADE (not the least gay of the company). You know, old fellow, you make it very difficult for us to embark upon this adventure in the proper eerie spirit.

DEARTH. Well, I'm for the garden.

(He walks to the window, and the others are going out by the door. But they do not go. There is a hitch somewhere--at the window apparently, for DEARTH, having begun to draw the curtains apart lets them fall, like one who has had a shock. The others remember long afterwards his grave face as he came quietly back and put his cigar on the table. The room is in darkness save for the light from one lamp.)

PURDIE (wondering). How, now, Dearth?

DEARTH. What is it we get in that wood, Lob?

ALICE. Ah, he won't tell us that.

LOB (shrinking). Come on!

ALICE (impressed by the change that has come over her husband). Tell us first.

LOB (forced to the disclosure). They say that in the wood you get what nearly everybody here is longing for--a second chance.

(The ladies are simultaneously enlightened.)

JOANNA (speaking for all). So that is what we have in common!

COADE: (with gentle regret). I have often thought, Coady, that if I had a second chance I should be a useful man instead of just a nice lazy one.

ALICE (morosely). A second chance!

LOB. Come on.

PURDIE (gaily). Yes, to the wood--the wood!

DEARTH (as they are going out by the door). Stop, why not go this way?

(He pulls the curtains apart, and there comes a sudden indrawing of breath from all, for no garden is there now. In its place is an endless wood of great trees; the nearest of them has come close to the window. It is a sombre wood, with splashes of moonshine and of blackness standing very still in it.

The party in the drawing-room are very still also; there is scarcely a cry or a movement. It is perhaps strange that the most obviously frightened is LOB who calls vainly for MATEY. The first articulate voice is DEARTH'S.)

DEARTH (very quietly). Any one ready to risk it?

PURDIE (after another silence). Of course there is nothing in it--just

DEARTH (grimly). Of course. Going out, Purdie?

(PURDIE draws back.)

MRS. DEARTH (the only one who is undaunted). A second chance! (She is looking at her husband. They all look at him as if he had been a leader once.)

DEARTH (with his sweet mournful smile). I shall be back in a moment--probably.

(As he passes into the wood his hands rise, as if a hammer had tapped him on the forehead. He is soon lost to view.)

LADY CAROLINE (after a long pause). He does not come back.

MRS. COADE. It's horrible.

(She steals off by the door to her room, calling to her husband to do likewise. He takes a step after her, and stops in the grip of the two words that holds them all. The stillness continues. At last MRS. PURDIE goes out into the wood, her hands raised, and is swallowed up by it.)

PURDIE. Mabel!

ALICE (sardonically). You will have to go now, Mr. Purdie.

(He looks at JOANNA, and they go out together, one tap of the hammer for each.)

LOB. That's enough. (Warningly.) Don't you go, Mrs. Dearth. You'll catch it if you go.

ALICE. A second chance!

(She goes out unflinching.)

LADY CAROLINE. One would like to know.

(She goes out. MRS. COADE'S voice is heard from the stair calling to her husband. He hesitates but follows LADY CAROLINE. To LOB now alone comes MATEY with a tray of coffee cups.)

MATEY (as he places his tray on the table). It is past your bed-time, sir. Say good-night to the ladies, and come along.

LOB. Matey, look!

(MATEY looks.)

MATEY (shrinking). Great heavens, then it's true!

LOB. Yes, but I--I wasn't sure.

(MATEY approaches the window cautiously to peer out, and his master gives him a sudden push that propels him into the wood. LOB's back is toward us as he stands alone staring out upon the unknown. He is terrified still; yet quivers of rapture are running up and down his little frame.)

# ACT II

We are translated to the depths of the wood in the enchantment of a moonlight night. In some other glade a nightingale is singing, in this one, in proud motoring attire, recline two mortals whom we have known in different conditions; the second chance has converted them into husband and wife. The man, of gross muddy build, lies luxurious on his back exuding affluence, a prominent part of him heaving playfully, like some little wave that will not rest in a still sea. A handkerchief over his face conceals from us what Colossus he may be, but his mate is our Lady Caroline. The nightingale trills on, and Lady Caroline takes up its song.

LADY CAROLINE. Is it not a lovely night, Jim. Listen, my own, to Philomel; he is saying that he is lately married. So are we, you ducky thing. I feel, Jim, that I am Rosalind and that you are my Orlando.

(The handkerchief being removed MR. MATEY is revealed; and the nightingale seeks some farther tree.)

MATEY. What do you say I am, Caroliny?

LADY CAROLINE (clapping her hands). My own one, don't you think it would he fun if we were to write poems about each other and pin them on the tree trunks?

MATEY (tolerantly). Poems? I never knew such a lass for high-flown language.

LADY CAROLINE. Your lass, dearest. Jim's lass.

MATEY (pulling her ear). And don't you forget it.

LADY CAROLINE (with the curiosity of woman). What would you do if I were to forget it, great bear?

MATEY. Take a stick to you.

LADY CAROLINE (so proud of him). I love to hear you talk like that; it is so virile. I always knew that it was a master I needed.

MATEY. It's what you all need.

LADY CAROLINE. It is, it is, you knowing wretch.

MATEY. Listen, Caroliny. (He touches his money pocket, which emits a crinkly sound--the squeak of angels.) That is what gets the ladies.

LADY CAROLINE. How much have you made this week, you wonderful man?

MATEY (blandly). Another two hundred or so. That's all, just two hundred or so.

LADY CAROLINE (caressing her wedding ring). My dear golden fetter, listen to him. Kiss my fetter, Jim.

MATEY. Wait till I light this cigar.

LADY CAROLINE. Let me hold the darling match.

MATEY. Tidy-looking Petitey Corona, this. There was a time when one of that sort would have run away with two days of my screw.

LADY CAROLINE. How I should have loved, Jim, to know you when you were poor. Fancy your having once been a clerk.

MATEY (remembering Napoleon and others). We all have our beginnings. But it wouldn't have mattered how I began, Caroliny: I should have come to the top just the same. (*Becoming a poet himself.*) I am a climber and there are nails in my boots for the parties beneath me. Boots! I tell you if I had been a bootmaker, I should have been the first bootmaker in London.

LADY CAROLINE (*a humourist at last*). I am sure you would, Jim; but should you have made the best boots?

MATEY (*uxoriously wishing that others could have heard this*). Very good. Caroliny; that is the nearest thing I have heard you say. But it's late; we had best be strolling back to our Rolls-Royce.

LADY CAROLINE (*as they rise*). I do hope the ground wasn't damp.

MATEY. Don't matter if it was; I was lying on your rug.

(*Indeed we notice now that he has had all the rug, and she the bare ground. JOANNA reaches the glade, now an unhappy lady who has got what she wanted. She is in country dress and is unknown to them as they are to her.*) Who is the mournful party?

JOANNA (*hesitating*). I wonder, sir, whether you happen to have seen my husband? I have lost him in the wood.

MATEY. We are strangers in these parts ourselves, missis. Have we passed any one, Caroliny?

LADY CAROLINE (*coyly*). Should we have noticed, dear? Might it be that old gent over there? (*After the delightful manner of those happily wed she has already picked up many of her lover's favourite words and phrases.*)

JOANNA. Oh no, my husband is quite young.

(*The woodlander referred to is MR COADE in gala costume; at his mouth a whistle he has made him from some friendly twig. To its ravishing music he is seen pirouetting charmingly among the trees, his new occupation.*)

MATEY (*signing to the unknown that he is wanted*). Seems a merry old cock. Evening to you, sir. Do you happen to have seen a young gentleman in the wood lately, all by himself, and looking for his wife?

COADE (*with a flourish of his legs*). Can't say I have.

JOANNA (*dolefully*). He isn't necessarily by himself; and I don't know- that he is looking for me. There may be a young lady with him.

(*The more happily married lady smiles, and Joanna is quick to take offence.*)

JOANNA. What do you mean by that?   LADY CAROLINE (neatly). Oho--if you like that better.

MATEY. Now, now, now--your manners, Caroliny.

COADE. Would he be singing or dancing?

JOANNA. Oh no--at least, I hope not.

COADE (an artist to the tips). Hope not? Odd! If he is doing neither I am not likely to notice him, but if I do, what name shall I say?

JOANNA (gloating not). Purdie; I am Mrs. Purdie.

COADE. I will try to keep a look-out, and if I see him . . . but I am rather occupied at present . . . (The reference is to his legs and a new step they are acquiring. He sways this way and that, and, whistle to lips, minuets off in the direction of Paradise.)

JOANNA (looking elsewhere). I am sorry I troubled you. I see him now.

LADY CAROLINE. Is he alone?

(JOANNA glares at her.)

Ah, I see from your face that he isn't.

MATEY (who has his wench in training). Caroliny, no awkward questions. Evening, missis, and I hope you will get him to go along with you quietly. (Looking after COADE.) Watch the old codger dancing.

(Light-hearted as children they dance after him, while JOANNA behind a tree awaits her lord. PURDIE in knickerbockers approaches with misgivings to make sure that his JOANNA is not in hiding, and then he gambols joyously with a charming confection whose name is MABEL. They chase each other from tree to tree, but fortunately not round JOANNA'S tree.)

MABEL (as he catches her). No, and no, and no. I don't know you nearly well enough for that. Besides, what would your wife say! I shall begin to think you are a very dreadful man, Mr. Purdie.

PURDIE (whose sincerity is not to be questioned). Surely you might call me Jack by this time.

MABEL (heaving). Perhaps, if you are very good, Jack.

PURDIE (of noble thoughts compact). If only Joanna were more like you.

MABEL. Like me? You mean her face? It is a--well, if it is not precisely pretty, it is a good face. (Handsomely.) I don't mind her face at all. I am glad you have got such a dependable little wife, Jack.

PURDIE (gloomily). Thanks.

MABEL (seated with a moonbeam in her lap). What would Joanna have said if she had seen you just now?

PURDIE. A wife should be incapable of jealousy.

MABEL Joanna jealous? But has she any reason? Jack, tell me, who is the woman?

PURDIE (restraining himself by a mighty effort, for he wishes always to be true to JOANNA). Shall I, Mabel, shall I?

MABEL (faltering, yet not wholly giving up the chase). I can't think who she is. Have I ever seen her?

PURDIE. Every time you look in a mirror.

MABEL (with her head on one side). How odd, Jack, that can't be; when I look in a mirror I see only myself.

PURDIE (gloating). How adorably innocent you are, Mabel. Joanna would have guessed at once.

(Slowly his meaning comes to her, and she is appalled.)

MABEL. Not that!

PURDIE (aflame). Shall I tell you now?

MABEL (palpitating exquisitely). I don't know, I am not sure. Jack, try not to say it, but if you feel you must, say it in such a way that it would not hurt the feelings of Joanna if she happened to be passing by, as she nearly always is.

(A little moan from JOANNA'S tree is unnoticed.)

PURDIE. I would rather not say it at all than that way. (He is touchingly anxious that she should know him as he really is.) I don't know, Mabel, whether you have noticed that I am not like other men. (He goes deeply into the very structure of his being.) All my life I have been a soul that has had to walk alone. Even as a child I had no hope that it would be otherwise. I distinctly remember when I was six thinking how unlike other children I was. Before I was twelve I suffered from terrible self-depreciation; I do so still. I suppose there never was a man who had a more lowly opinion of himself.

MABEL. Jack, you who are so universally admired.

PURDIE. That doesn't help; I remain my own judge. I am afraid I am a dark spirit, Mabel. Yes, yes, my dear, let me leave nothing untold however it may damage me in your eyes. Your eyes! I cannot remember a time when I did not think of Love as a great consuming passion; I visualised it, Mabel, as perhaps few have done, but always as the abounding joy that could come to others but never to me. I expected too much of women: I suppose I was touched to finer issues than most. That has been my tragedy.

MABEL. Then you met Joanna.

PURDIE. Then I met Joanna. Yes! Foolishly, as I now see, I thought she would understand that I was far too deep a nature really to mean the little things I sometimes said to her. I suppose a man was never placed in such a position before. What was I to do? Remember, I was always certain that the ideal love could never come to me. Whatever the circumstances, I was convinced that my soul must walk alone.

MABEL. Joanna, how could you.

PURDIE (firmly). Not a word against her, Mabel; if blame there is the blame is mine.

MABEL. And so you married her.

PURDIE. And so I married her.

MABEL. Out of pity.

PURDIE. I felt it was a man's part. I was such a child in worldly matters that it was pleasant to me to have the right to pay a woman's bills; I enjoyed seeing her garments lying about on my chairs. In time that exultation wore off. But I was not unhappy, I didn't expect much, I was always so sure that no woman could ever plumb the well of my emotions.

MABEL. Then you met me.

PURDIE. Then I met you.

MABEL. Too late--never--forever--forever--never. They are the saddest words in the English tongue.

PURDIE. At the time I thought a still sadder word was Joanna.

MABEL. What was it you saw in me that made you love me?

PURDIE (plumbing the well of his emotions). I think it was the feeling that you are so like myself.

MABEL (with great eyes). Have you noticed that, Jack? Sometimes it has almost terrified me.

PURDIE. We think the same thoughts; we are not two, Mabel; we are one. Your hair--

MABEL. Joanna knows you admire it, and for a week she did hers in the same way.

PURDIE. I never noticed.

MABEL. That was why she gave it up. And it didn't really suit her. (Ruminating.) I can't think of a good way of doing dear Joanna's hair. What is that you are muttering to yourself, Jack? Don't keep anything from me.

PURDIE. I was repeating a poem I have written: it is in two words, 'Mabel Purdie.' May I teach it to you, sweet: say 'Mabel Purdie' to me.

MABEL (timidly covering his mouth with her little hand). If I were to say it, Jack, I should be false to Joanna: never ask me to be that. Let us go on.

PURDIE (merciless in his passion). Say it, Mabel, say it. See I write it on the ground with your sunshade.

MABEL. If it could be! Jack, I'll whisper it to you.

(She is whispering it as they wander, not two but one, farther into the forest, ardently believing in themselves; they are not hypocrites. The somewhat bedraggled figure of Joanna follows them, and the nightingale resumes his love-song. 'That's all you know, you bird!' thinks Joanna cynically. The nightingale, however, is not singing for them nor for her, but for another pair he has espied below. They are racing, the prize to be for the one who first finds the spot where the easel was put up last night. The hobbledehoy is sure to be the winner, for she is less laden, and the father loses time by singing as he comes. Also she is. all legs and she started ahead. Brambles adhere to her, one boot has been in the water and she has as many freckles as there are stars in heaven. She is as lovely as you think she is, and she is aged the moment when you like your daughter best. A hoot of triumph from her brings her father to the spot.)

MARGARET. Daddy, Daddy. I have won. Here is the place. Crack-in-my-eye-Tommy!

(He comes. Crack-in-my-eye-Tommy, this engaging fellow in tweeds is MR. DEARTH, ablaze in happiness and health and a daughter. He finishes his song, picked up in the Latin Quarter.)

DEARTH. Yes, that is the tree I stuck my easel under last night, and behold the blessed moon behaving more gorgeously than ever. I am sorry to have kept you waiting, old moon; but you ought to know by now how time passes. Now, keep still, while I hand you down to posterity.

(The easel is erected, MARGARET helping by getting in the way.)

MARGARET (critical, as an artist's daughter should be.) The moon is rather pale to-night, isn't she?

DEARTH. Comes of keeping late hours.

MARGARET (showing off). Daddy, watch me, look at me. Please, sweet moon, a pleasant expression. No, no, not as if you were sitting or it; that is too professional. That is better; thank you. Now keep it. That is the sort of thing you say to them, Dad.

DEARTH (quickly at work). I oughtn't to have brought you out so late; you should be tucked up in your cosy bed at home.

MARGARET (pursuing a squirrel that isn't there). With the pillow anyhow.

DEARTH. Except in its proper place.

MARGARET (wetting the other foot). And the sheet over my face.

DEARTH. Where it oughtn't to be.

MARGARET (more or less upside down). And Daddy tiptoeing in to take it off.

DEARTH. Which is more than you deserve.

MARGARET (in a tree). Then why does he stand so long at the door? And before he has gone she bursts out laughing, for she has been awake all the time.

DEARTH. That's about it. What a life! But I oughtn't to have brought you here. Best to have the sheet over you when the moon is about; moonlight is bad for little daughters.

MARGARET (pelting him with nuts). I can't sleep when the moon's at the full; she keeps calling to me to get up. Perhaps I am *her* daughter too.

DEARTH. Gad, you look it to-night.

MARGARET. Do I? Then can't you paint me into the picture as well as Mamma? You could call it 'A Mother and Daughter' or simply 'Two ladies.' if the moon thinks that calling me her daughter would make her seem too old.

DEARTH. O matre pulchra filia pulchrior. That means, 'O Moon--more beautiful than any twopenny-halfpenny daughter.'

MARGARET (emerging in an unexpected place). Daddy, do you really prefer her?

DEARTH. 'Sh! She's not a patch on you; it's the sort of thing we say to our sitters to keep them in good humour. (He surveys ruefully a great stain on her frock.) I wish to heaven, Margaret, we were not both so fond of apple-tart. And what's this? (Catching hold of her skirt.)

MARGARET (unnecessarily). It's a tear.

DEARTH. I should think it is a tear.

MARGARET. That boy at the farm did it. He kept calling Snubs after me, but I got him down and kicked him in the stomach. He is rather a jolly boy.

DEARTH. He sounds it. Ye Gods, what a night!

MARGARET (considering the picture). And what a moon! Dad, she is not quite so fine as that.

DEARTH. 'Sh! I have touched her up.

MARGARET. Dad, Dad--what a funny man!

(She has seen MR. COADE with whistle, enlivening the wood. He pirouettes round them and departs to add to the happiness of others. MARGARET gives an excellent imitation of him at which her father shakes his head, then reprehensibly joins in the dance. Her mood changes, she clings to him.)

MARGARET. Hold me tight, Daddy, I 'm frightened. I think they want to take you away from me.

DEARTH. Who, gosling?

MARGARET. I don't know. It's too lovely, Daddy; I won't be able to keep hold of it.

DEARTH. What is?

MARGARET. The world--everything--and you, Daddy, most of all. Things that are too beautiful can't last.

DEARTH (who knows it). Now, how did you find that out?

MARGARET (still in his arms). I don't know, Daddy, am I sometimes stranger than other people's daughters?

DEARTH. More of a madcap, perhaps.

MARGARET (solemnly). Do you think I am sometimes too full of gladness?

DEARTH. My sweetheart, you do sometimes run over with it. (He is at his easel again.)

MARGARET (persisting). To be very gay, dearest dear, is so near to being very sad.

DEARTH (who knows it). How did you find that out, child?

MARGARET. I don't know. From something in me that's afraid. (Unexpectedly.) Daddy, what is a 'might-have-been?'

DEARTH. A might-have-been? They are ghosts, Margaret. I daresay I 'might have been' a great swell of a painter, instead of just this uncommonly happy nobody. Or again, I might have been a worthless idle waster of a fellow.

MARGARET (laughing). You!  DEARTH. Who knows? Some little kink in me might have set me off on the wrong road. And that poor soul I might so easily have been might have had no Margaret. My word, I'm sorry for him.

MARGARET. So am I. (She conceives a funny picture.) The poor old Daddy, wandering about the world without me!

DEARTH. And there are other 'might-have-beens'--lovely ones, but intangible. Shades, Margaret, made of sad folk's thoughts.

MARGARET (jigging about). I am so glad I am not a shade. How awful it would be, Daddy, to wake up and find one wasn't alive.

DEARTH. It would, dear.

MARGARET. Daddy, wouldn't it be awful. I think men need daughters.

DEARTH. They do.

MARGARET. Especially artists.

DEARTH. Yes, especially artists.

MARGARET. Especially artists.

DEARTH. Especially artists.

MARGARET (covering herself with leaves and kicking them off). Fame is not everything.

DEARTH. Fame is rot; daughters are the thing.

MARGARET. Daughters are the thing.

DEARTH. Daughters are the thing.

MARGARET. I wonder if sons would be even nicer?

DEARTH. Not a patch on daughters. The awful thing about a son is that never, never--at least, from the day he goes to school--can you tell him that you rather like him. By the time he is ten you can't even take him on your knee. Sons are not worth having, Margaret. Signed W. Dearth.

MARGARET. But if you were a mother, Dad, I daresay he would let you do it.

DEARTH. Think so?

MARGARET. I mean when no one was looking. Sons are not so bad. Signed, M. Dearth. But I'm glad you prefer daughters. (She works her way toward him on her knees, making the tear larger.) At what age are we nicest, Daddy? (She has constantly to repeat her questions, he is so engaged with his moon.) Hie, Daddy, at what age are we nicest? Daddy, hie, hie, at what age are we nicest?

DEARTH. Eh? That's a poser. I think you were nicest when you were two and knew your alphabet up to G but fell over at H. No, you were best when you were half-past three; or just before you struck six; or in the mumps year, when I asked you in the early morning how you were and you said solemnly 'I haven't tried yet.'

MARGARET (awestruck). Did I?

DEARTH. Such was your answer. (Struggling with the momentous question.) But I am not sure that chicken-pox doesn't beat mumps. Oh Lord, I'm all wrong. The nicest time in a father's life is the year before she puts up her hair.

MARGARET (topheavy with pride in herself). I suppose that is a splendid time. But there's a nicer year coming to you. Daddy, there is a nicer year coming to you.

DEARTH. Is there, darling?

MARGARET. Daddy, the year she does put up her hair!

DEARTH. (with arrested brush). Puts it up for ever? You know, I am afraid that when the day for that comes I shan't be able to stand it. It will be too exciting. My poor heart, Margaret.

MARGARET (rushing at him). No, no, it will be lucky you, for it isn't to be a bit like that. I am to be a girl and woman day about for the first year. You will never know which I am till you look at my hair. And even then you won't know, for if it is down I shall put it up, and if it is up I shall put it down. And so my Daddy will gradually get used to the idea.

DEARTH. (wryly). I see you have been thinking it out.

MARGARET (gleaming). I have been doing more than that. Shut your eyes, Dad, and I shall give you a glimpse into the future.

DEARTH. I don't know that I want that: the present is so good.

MARGARET. Shut your eyes, please.

DEARTH. No, Margaret.

MARGARET. Please, Daddy.

DEARTH. Oh, all right. They are shut.

MARGARET. Don't open them till I tell you. What finger is that?

DEARTH. The dirty one.

MARGARET (on her knees among the leaves). Daddy, now I am putting up my hair. I have got such a darling of a mirror. It is such a darling mirror I 've got, Dad. Dad, don't look. I shall tell you about it. It is a little pool of water. I wish we could take it home and hang it up. Of course the moment my hair is up there will be other changes also; for instance, I shall talk quite differently.

DEARTH. Pooh. Where are my matches, dear?

MARGARET, Top pocket, waistcoat.

DEARTH (trying to light his pipe in darkness). You were meaning to frighten me just now.

MARGARET. No. I am just preparing you. You see, darling, I can't call you Dad when my hair is up. I think I shall call you Parent. (He growls.) Parent dear, do you remember the days when your Margaret was a slip of a girl, and sat on your knee? How foolish we were, Parent, in those distant days.

DEARTH. Shut up, Margaret.

MARGARET. Now I must be more distant to you; more like a boy who could not sit on your knee any more.

DEARTH. See here, I want to go on painting. Shall I look now?

MARGARET. I am not quite sure whether I want you to. It makes such a difference. Perhaps you won't know me. Even the pool is looking a little scared. (The change in her voice makes him open his eyes quickly. She confronts him shyly.) What do you think? Will I do?

DEARTH. Stand still, dear, and let me look my fill. The Margaret that is to be.

MARGARET (the change in his voice falling clammy on her). You'll see me often enough, Daddy, like this, so you don't need to look your fill. You are looking as long as if this were to be the only time.

DEARTH. (with an odd tremor). Was I? Surely it isn't to be that.

MARGARET. Be gay, Dad. (Bumping into him and round him and over him.) You will be sick of Margaret with her hair up before you are done with her.

DEARTH. I expect so.

MARGARET. Shut up, Daddy. (She waggles her head, and down comes her hair.) Daddy, I know what you are thinking of. You are thinking what a handful she is going to be.

DEARTH. Well, I guess she is.

MARGARET (surveying him from another angle). Now you are thinking about--about my being in love some day.

DEARTH (with unnecessary warmth). Rot!

MARGARET (reassuringly). I won't, you know; no, never. Oh, I have quite decided, so don't be afraid, (Disordering his hair.) Will you hate him at first, Daddy? Daddy, will you hate him? Will you hate him, Daddy?

DEARTH (at work). Whom?

MARGARET. Well, if there was?

DEARTH. If there was what, darling?

MARGARET. You know the kind of thing I mean, quite well. Would you hate him at first?

DEARTH. I hope not. I should want to strangle him, but I wouldn't hate him.

MARGARET. *I* would. That is to say, if I liked him.

DEARTH. If you liked him how could you hate him?

MARGARET. For daring!

DEARTH. Daring what?

MARTARET. You know. (Sighing.) But of course I shall have no say in the matter. You will do it all. You do everything for me.

DEARTH (with a groan). I can't help it.

MARGARET. You will even write my love-letters, if I ever have any to write, which I won't.

DEARTH (ashamed). Surely to goodness, Margaret, I will leave you alone to do that!

MARGARET. Not you; you will try to, but you won't be able.

DEARTH (in a hopeless attempt at self-defence). I want you, you see, to do everything exquisitely. I do wish I could leave you to do things a little more for yourself. I suppose it's owing to my having had to be father and mother both. I knew nothing practically about the bringing up of children, and of course I couldn't trust you to a nurse.

MARGARET (severely). Not you; so sure you could do it better yourself. That's you all over. Daddy, do you remember how you taught me to balance a biscuit on my nose, like a puppy?

DEARTH (sadly). Did I?

MARGARET. You called me Rover.

DEARTH. I deny that.

MARGARET. And when you said 'snap' I caught the biscuit in my mouth.

DEARTH. Horrible.

MARGARET (gleaming). Daddy, I can do it still! (Putting a biscuit on her nose.) Here is the last of my supper. Say 'snap,' Daddy.

DEARTH. Not I.

MARGARET. Say 'snap,' please.

DEARTH. I refuse.

MARGARET. Daddy!

DEARTH. Snap. (She catches the biscuit in her mouth.) Let that be the last time, Margaret.

MARGARET. Except just once more. I don't mean now, but when my hair is really up. If I should ever have a--a Margaret of my own, come in and see me, Daddy, in my white bed, and say 'snap'--and I'll have the biscuit ready.

DEARTH (turning away his head). Right O.

MARGARET. Dad, if I ever should marry, not that I will but if I should--at the marriage ceremony will you let me be the one who says 'I do'?

DEARTH. I suppose I deserve this.

MARGARET (coaxingly). You think I 'm pretty, don't you, Dad, whatever other people say?

DEARTH. Not so bad.

MARGARET. I *know* I have nice ears.

DEARTH. They are all right now, but I had to work on them for months.

MARGARET. You don't mean to say that you did my ears?

DEARTH. Rather!

MARGARET (grown humble). My dimple is my own.

DEARTH. I am glad you think so. I wore out the point of my little finger over that dimple.

MARGARET. Even my dimple! Have I anything that is really mine? A bit of my nose or anything?   DEARTH. When you were a babe you had a laugh that was all your own.

MARGARET. Haven't I it now?

DEARTH. It's gone. (He looks ruefully at her.) I'll tell you how it went. We were fishing in a stream--that is to say, I was wading and you were sitting on my shoulders holding the rod. We didn't catch anything. Somehow or another--I can't think how I did it--you irritated me, and I answered you sharply.

MARGARET (gasping). I can't believe that.

DEARTH. Yes, it sounds extraordinary, but I did. It gave you a shock, and, for the moment, the world no longer seemed a safe place to you; your faith in me had always made it safe till then. You were suddenly not even sure of your bread and butter, and a frightened tear came to your eyes. I was in a nice state about it, I can tell you. (He is in a nice state about it still.)

MARGARET. Silly! (Bewildered) But what has that to do with my laugh, Daddy?

DEARTH. The laugh that children are born with lasts just so long as they have perfect faith. To think that it was I who robbed you of yours!

MARGARET. Don't, dear. I am sure the laugh just went off with the tear to comfort it, and they have been playing about that stream ever since. They have quite forgotten us, so why should we remember them. Cheeky little beasts!  Shall I tell you my farthest back recollection? (In some awe.) I remember the first time I saw the stars. I had never seen night, and then I saw it and the stars together. Crack-in-my-eye Tommy, it isn't every one who can boast of such a lovely, lovely, recollection for their earliest, is it?

DEARTH. I was determined your earliest should be a good one.

MARGARET (blankly). Do you mean to say you planned it?

DEARTH. Rather! Most people's earliest recollection is of some trivial thing; how they cut their finger, or lost a piece of string. I was resolved my Margaret's should be something bigger. I was poor, but I could give her the stars.

MARGARET (clutching him round the legs). Oh, how you love me, Daddikins.

DEARTH. Yes, I do, rather.

(A vagrant woman has wandered in their direction, one whom the shrill winds of life have lashed and bled; here and there ragged graces still cling to her, and unruly passion smoulders, but she, once a dear, fierce rebel, with eyes of storm, is now first of all a whimperer. She and they meet as strangers.)

MARGARET (nicely, as becomes an artist's daughter.) Good evening.

ALICE. Good evening, Missy; evening, Mister.

DEARTH (seeing that her eyes search the ground). Lost anything?

ALICE. Sometimes when the tourists have had their sandwiches there are bits left over, and they squeeze them between the roots to keep the place tidy. I am looking for bits.

DEARTH. You don't tell me you are as hungry as that?

ALICE (with spirit). Try me. (Strange that he should not know that once loved husky voice.)

MARGARET (rushing at her father and feeling all his pockets.) Daddy, that was my last biscuit!

DEARTH. We must think of something else.

MARGARET (taking her hand). Yes, wait a bit, we are sure to think of something. Daddy, think of something.

ALICE (sharply). Your father doesn't like you to touch the likes of me.

MARGARET. Oh yes, he does. (Defiantly) And if he didn't, I'd do it all the same. This is a bit of *myself*, daddy.

DEARTH. That is all you know.

ALICE (whining). You needn't be angry with her. Mister; I'm all right.

DEARTH. I am not angry with her; I am very sorry for you.

ALICE (flaring). if I had my rights, I would be as good as you--and better.

DEARTH. I daresay.

ALICE. I have had men-servants and a motor-car.  DEARTH. Margaret and I never rose to that.

MARGARET (stung). I have been in a taxi several times, and Dad often gets telegrams.

DEARTH. Margaret!

MARGARET. I'm sorry I boasted.

ALICE. That's nothing. I have a town house--at least I had . . . At any rate he said there was a town house.

MARGARET (interested). Fancy his not knowing for certain.

ALICE. The Honourable Mrs. Finch-Fallowe--that's who I am.

MARGARET (cordially). It's a lovely name.

ALICE. Curse him.

MARGARET. Don't you like him?

DEARTH. We won't go into that. I have nothing to do with your past, but I wish we had some food to offer you.

ALICE. You haven't a flask?

DEARTH. No, I don't take anything myself. But let me see. . . .

MARGARET (sparkling). I know! You said we had five pounds. (To the needy one.) Would you like five pounds?

DEARTH. Darling, don't be stupid; we haven't paid our bill at the inn.

ALICE (with bravado). All right; I never asked you for anything.

DEARTH. Don't take me up in that way: I have had my ups and downs myself. Here is ten bob and welcome.

(He surreptitiously slips a coin into MARGARET'S hand.)

MARGARET. And I have half a crown. It is quite easy for us. Dad will be getting another fiver any day. You can't think how exciting it is when the fiver comes in; we dance and then we run out and buy chops.

DEARTH. Margaret!

ALICE. It's kind of you. I'm richer this minute than I have been for many a day.

DEARTH. It's nothing; I am sure you would do the same for us.

ALICE. I wish I was as sure.

DEARTH. Of course you would. Glad to be of any help. Get some victuals as quickly as you can. Best of wishes, ma'am, and may your luck change.

ALICE. Same to you, and may yours go on.

MARGARET. Good-night.

ALICE. What is her name, Mister?

DEARTH (who has returned to his easel). Margaret.

ALICE. Margaret. You drew something good out of the lucky bag when you got her, Mister.

DEARTH. Yes.

ALICE. Take care of her; they are easily lost.

(She shuffles away.)

DEARTH. Poor soul. I expect she has had a rough time, and that some man is to blame for it--partly, at any rate. (Restless) That woman rather affects me, Margaret; I don't know why. Didn't you like her husky voice? (He goes on painting.) I say, Margaret, we lucky ones, let's swear always to be kind to people who are down on their luck, and then when we are kind let's be a little kinder.

MARGARET (gleefully). Yes, let's.

DEARTH. Margaret, always feel sorry for the failures, the ones who are always failures--especially in my sort of calling. Wouldn't it be lovely, to turn them on the thirty-ninth year of failure into glittering successes?

MARGARET. Topping.

DEARTH. Topping.

MARGARET. Oh, topping. How could we do it, Dad?

DEARTH. By letter. 'To poor old Tom Broken Heart, Top Attic, Garret Chambers, S.E.--'DEAR SIR,--His Majesty has been graciously pleased to purchase your superb picture of Marlow Ferry.'

MARGARET. 'P.S.--I am sending the money in a sack so as you can hear it chink.'

DEARTH. What could we do for our friend who passed just now? I can't get her out of my head.

MARGARET. You have made me forget her. (Plaintively) Dad, I didn't like it.

DEARTH. Didn't like what, dear?

MARGARET (shuddering). I didn't like her saying that about your losing me.

DEARTH (the one thing of which he is sure). I shan't lose you.

MARGARET (hugging his arm). It would be hard for me if you lost me, but it would be worse for you. I don't know how I know that, but I do know it. What would you do without me?

DEARTH (almost sharply). Don't talk like that, dear. It is wicked and stupid, and naughty. Somehow that poor woman--I won't paint any more to-night.

MARGARET. Let's get out of the wood; it frightens me.

DEARTH. And you loved it a moment ago. Hullo! (He has seen a distant blurred light in the wood, apparently from a window.) I hadn't noticed there was a house there.

MARGARET (tingling). Daddy, I feel sure there wasn't a house there!

DEARTH. Goose. It is just that we didn't look: our old way of letting the world go hang; so interested in ourselves. Nice behaviour for people who have been boasting about what they would do for other people. Now I see what I ought to do.

MARGARET. Let's get out of the wood.

DEARTH. Yes, but my idea first. It is to rouse these people and get food from them for the husky one.

MARGARET (clinging to him). She is too far away now.

DEARTH. I can overtake her.

MARGARET (in a frenzy). Don't go into that house, Daddy! I don't know why it is, but I am afraid of that house!

(He waggles a reproving finger at her.)

DEARTH. There is a kiss for each moment until I come back. (She wipes them from her face.) Oh, naughty, go and stand in the corner. (She stands against a tree but she stamps her foot.) Who has got a nasty temper!

(She tries hard not to smile, but she smiles and he smiles, and they make comic faces at each other, as they have done in similar circumstances since she first opened her eyes.)

I shall be back before you can count a hundred.

(He goes off humming his song so that she may still hear him when he is lost to sight; all just as so often before. She tries dutifully to count her hundred, but the wood grows dark and soon she is afraid again. She runs from tree to tree calling to her Daddy. We begin to lose her among the shadows.)

MARGARET (Out of the impalpable that is carrying her away). Daddy, come back; I don't want to be a might-have-been.

# ACT III

Lob's room has gone very dark as it sits up awaiting the possible return of the adventurers. The curtains are drawn, so that no light comes from outside. There is a tapping on the window, and anon two intruders are stealing about the floor, with muffled cries when they meet unexpectedly. They find the switch and are revealed as Purdie and his Mabel. Something has happened to them as they emerged from the wood, but it is so superficial that neither notices it: they are again in the evening dress in which they had left the house. But they are still being led by that strange humour of the blood.

MABEL (looking around her curiously). A pretty little room; I wonder who is the owner?

PURDIE. It doesn't matter; the great thing is that we have escaped Joanna.

MABEL. Jack, look, a man!

(The term may not be happily chosen, but the person indicated is Lob curled up on his chair by a dead fire. The last look on his face before he fell asleep having been a leery one it is still there.)

PURDIE. He is asleep.

MABEL. Do you know him?

PURDIE. Not I. Excuse me, sir, Hi! (No shaking, however, wakens the sleeper.)

MABEL. Darling, how extraordinary.

PURDIE (always considerate). After all, precious, have we any right to wake up a stranger, just to tell him that we are runaways hiding in his house?

MABEL (who comes of a good family). I think he would expect it of us.

PURDIE (after trying again). There is no budging him.

MABEL (appeased). At any rate, we have done the civil thing.

(She has now time to regard the room more attentively, including the tray of coffee cups which MATEY had left on the table in a not unimportant moment of his history.) There have evidently been people here, but they haven't drunk their coffee. Ugh! cold as a deserted egg in a bird's nest. Jack, if you were a clever detective you could construct those people out of their neglected coffee cups. I wonder who they are and what has spirited them away?

PURDIE. Perhaps they have only gone to bed. Ought we to knock them up?

MABEL (after considering what her mother would have done). I think not, dear. I suppose we have run away, Jack--meaning to?

PURDIE (with the sturdiness that weaker vessels adore). Irrevocably. Mabel, if the dog-like devotion of a lifetime . . . (He becomes conscious that something has happened to LOB'S leer. It has not left his face but it has shifted.) He is not shamming, do you think?

MABEL. Shake him again.

PURDIE (after shaking him). It's all right. Mabel, if the dog-like devotion of a lifetime . . .

MABEL. Poor little Joanna! Still, if a woman insists on being a pendulum round a man's neck . . .

PURDIE. Do give me a chance, Mabel. If the dog-like devotion of a lifetime . . . (JOANNA comes through the curtains so inopportunely that for the moment he is almost pettish.)

May I say, this is just a little too much, Joanna!

JOANNA (unconscious as they of her return to her dinner gown). So, sweet husband, your soul is still walking alone, is it?

MABEL (who hates coarseness of any kind). How can you sneak about in this way, Joanna? Have you no pride?

JOANNA (dashing away a tear). Please to address me as Mrs. Purdie, madam. (She sees LOB.) Who is this man?

PURDIE. We don't know; and there is no waking him. You can try, if you like.

(Failing to rouse him JOANNA makes a third at table. They are all a little inconsequential, as if there were still some moon-shine in their hair.)

JOANNA. You were saying something about the devotion of a lifetime; please go on.

PURDIE (diffidently). I don't like to before you, Joanna.

JOANNA (becoming coarse again). Oh, don't mind me.

PURDIE (looking like a note of interrogation). I should certainly like to say it.

MABEL (loftily). And I shall be proud to hear it.

PURDIE. I should have liked to spare you this, Joanna; you wouldn't put your hands over your ears?

JOANNA (alas). No, sir.

MABEL. Fie, Joanna. Surely a wife's natural delicacy . . .

PURDIE (severely). As you take it in that spirit, Joanna, I can proceed with a clear conscience. If the dog-like devotion of a lifetime--(He reels a little, staring at LOB, over whose face the leer has been wandering like an insect.)

MABEL. Did he move?

PURDIE. It isn't that  I am feeling--very funny. Did one of you tap me just now on the forehead?

(Their hands also have gone to their foreheads.)

MABEL. I think I have been in this room before.

PURDIE (flinching). There is something coming rushing back to me.

MABEL. I seem to know that coffee set. If I do, the lid of the milk jug is chipped. It is!

JOANNA. I can't remember this man's name; but I am sure it begins with L.

MABEL. Lob.

PURDIE. Lob.

JOANNA. Lob.

PURDIE. Mabel, your dress?

MABEL (beholding it). How on earth . . . ?

JOANNA. My dress! (To PURDIE.) You were in knickerbockers in the wood.

PURDIE. And so I am now. (He sees he is not.) Where did I change? The wood! Let me think. The wood . . . the wood, certainly. But the wood wasn't the wood.

JOANNA (revolving like one in pursuit). My head is going round.

MABEL. Lob's wood! I remember it all. We were here. We did go.

PURDIE. So we did. But how could . . . ? where was . . . ?

JOANNE. And who was . . . ?

MABEL And what was . . . ?

PURDIE (even in this supreme hour a man). Don't let go. Hold on to what we were doing, or we shall lose grip of ourselves. Devotion. Something about devotion. Hold on to devotion. 'If the dog-like devotion of a lifetime . . . ' Which of you was

I saying that to?

MABEL. To me.

PURDIE. Are you sure?

MABEL (shakily). I am not quite sure.

PURDIE (anxiously). Joanna, what do you think? (With a sudden increase of uneasiness.) Which of you is my wife?

JOANNA (without enthusiasm). I am. No, I am not. It is Mabel who is your wife!

MABEL. Me?

PURDIE (with a curious gulp). Why, of course you are, Mabel!

MABEL. I believe I am!

PURDIE. And yet how can it be? I was running away with you.

JOANNA (solving that problem). You don't need to do it now.

PURDIE. The wood. Hold on to the wood. The wood is what explains it. Yes, I see the whole thing. (He gazes at LOB.) You infernal old rascal! Let us try to think it out. Don't any one speak for a moment. Think first. Love . . . Hold on to love. (He gets another tap.) I say, I believe I am not a deeply passionate chap at all; I believe I am just . . . . a philanderer!

MABEL. It is what you are.

JOANNA (more magnanimous). Mabel, what about ourselves?

PURDIE (to whom it is truly a nauseous draught). I didn't know. Just a philanderer! (The soul of him would like at this instant to creep into another body.) And if people don't change, I suppose we shall begin all over again now.

JOANNA (the practical). I daresay; but not with each other. I may philander again, but not with you.

(They look on themselves without approval, always a sorry occupation. The man feels it most because he has admired himself most, or perhaps partly for some better reason.)

PURDIE (saying good-bye to an old friend). John Purdie, John Purdie, the fine fellow I used to think you! (When he is able to look them in the face again.) The wood has taught me one thing, at any rate.

MABEL (dismally). What, Jack?

PURDIE. That it isn't accident that shapes our lives.

JOANNA. No, it's Fate.

PURDIE (the truth running through him, seeking for a permanent home in him, willing to give him still another chance, loth to desert him). It's not Fate, Joanna. Fate is something outside us. What really plays the dickens with us is some thing in ourselves. Something that makes us go on doing the same sort of fool things, however many chances we get.

MABEL. Something in ourselves?

PURDIE (shivering). Something we are born with.

JOANNA. Can't we cut out the beastly thing?

PURDIE. Depends, I expect, on how long we have pampered him. We can at least control him if we try hard enough. But I have for the moment an abominably clear perception that the likes of me never really tries. Forgive me, Joanna--no, Mabel--both of you. (He is a shamed man.) It isn't very pleasant to discover that one is a rotter. I suppose I shall get used to it.

JOANNA. I could forgive anybody anything to-night. (Candidly.) It is so lovely not to be married to you, Jack.

PURDIE (spiritless). I can understand that. I do feel small.

JOANNA (the true friend). You will soon swell up again.

PURDIE (for whom, alas, we need not weep). That is the appalling thing. But at present, at any rate, I am a rag at your feet, Joanna--no, at yours, Mabel. Are you going to pick me up? I don't advise it.

MABEL. I don't know whether I want to, Jack. To begin with, which of us is it your lonely soul is in search of?

JOANNA. Which of us is the fluid one, or the fluider one?

MABEL. Are you and I one? Or are you and Joanna one? Or are the three of us two?

JOANNA. He wants you to whisper in his ear, Mabel, the entrancing poem, 'Mabel Purdie.' Do it, Jack; there will be nothing wrong in it now.

PURDIE. Rub it in.

MABEL. When I meet Joanna's successor--

PURDIE (quailing). No, no, Mabel none of that. At least credit me with having my eyes open at last. There will be no more of this. I swear it by all that is--

JOANNA (in her excellent imitation of a sheep). Baa-a, he is off again.

PURDIE. Oh Lord, so I am.

MABEL. Don't, Joanna.

PURDIE (his mind still illumined). She is quite right--I was. In my present state of depression--which won't last--I feel there is something in me that will make me go on being the same ass, however many chances I get. I haven't the stuff in me to take warning. My whole being is corroded. Shakespeare knew what he was talking about--'The fault, dear Brutus, is not in our stars, But in ourselves, that we are underlings.'

JOANNA. For 'dear Brutus' we are to read 'dear audience' I suppose?

PURDIE. You have it.

JOANNA. Meaning that we have the power to shape ourselves?

PURDIE. We have the power right enough.

JOANNA. But isn't that rather splendid?

PURDIE. For those who have the grit in them, yes. (Still seeing with a strange clearness through the chink the hammer has made.) And they are not the dismal chappies; they are the ones with the thin bright faces. (He sits lugubriously by his wife and is sorry for the first time that she has not married a better man.) I am afraid there is not much fight in me, Mabel, but we shall see. If you catch me at it again, have the goodness to whisper to me in passing, 'Lob's Wood.' That may cure me for the time being.

MABEL (still certain that she loved him once but not so sure why.) Perhaps I will . . . as long as I care to bother, Jack. It depends on you how long that is to be.

JOANNA (to break an awkward pause). I feel that there is hope in that as well as a warning. Perhaps the wood may prove to have been useful after all. (This brighter view of the situation meets with no immediate response. With her next suggestion she reaches harbour.) You know, we are not people worth being sorrowful about--so let us laugh.

(The ladies succeed in laughing though not prettily, but the man has been too much shaken.)

JOANNA (in the middle of her laugh). We have forgotten the others! I wonder what is happening to them?

PURDIE (reviving). Yes, what about them? Have they changed!

MABEL. I didn't see any of them in the wood.

JOANNA. Perhaps we did see them without knowing them; we didn't know Lob.

PURDIE (daunted). That's true.

JOANNA. Won't it be delicious to be here to watch them when they come back, and see them waking up--or whatever it was we did.

PURDIE. What was it we did? I think something tapped me on the forehead.

MABEL (blanching). How do we know the others will come back?

JOANNA (infected). We don't know. How awful!

MABEL. Listen!

PURDIE. I distinctly hear some one on the stairs.

MABEL. It will be Matey.

PURDIE (the chink beginning to close). Be cautious both of you; don't tell him we have had any . . . odd experiences.

(It is, however, MRS. COADE who comes downstairs in a dressing-gown and carrying a candle and her husband's muffler.)

MRS. COADE. So you are back at last. A nice house, I must say. Where is Coady?

PURDIE (taken aback). Coady! Did he go into the wood, too?

MRS. COADE (placidly). I suppose so. I have been down several times to look for him.

MABEL. Coady, too!

JOANNA (seeing visions). I wonder . . . Oh, how dreadful!

MRS. COADE. What is dreadful, Joanna?

JOANNA (airily). Nothing. I was just wondering what he is doing.

MRS. COADE. Doing? What should he be doing? Did anything odd happen to you in the wood?

PURDIE (taking command). No, no, nothing.

JOANNA. We just strolled about, and came back. (That subject being exhausted she points to LOB). Have you noticed him?

MRS. COADE. Oh, yes; he has been like that all the time. A sort of stupor, I think; and sometimes the strangest grin comes over his face.

PURDIE (wincing). Grin?

MRS. COADE. Just as if he were seeing amusing things in his sleep.

PURDIE (guardedly). I daresay he is. Oughtn't we to get Matey to him?

MRS. COADE. Matey has gone, too.

PURDIE. Wha-at!

MRS. COADE. At all events he is not in the house.

JOANNA (unguardedly). Matey! I wonder who is with him.

MRS. COADE. Must somebody be with him?

JOANNA. Oh, no, not at all.

(They are simultaneously aware that someone outside has reached the window.)

MRS. COADE. I hope it is Coady.

(The other ladies are too fond of her to share this wish.)

MABEL. Oh, I hope not.

MRS. COADE (blissfully). Why, Mrs. Purdie?

JOANNA (coaxingly). Dear Mrs. Coade, whoever he is, and whatever he does, I beg you not to be surprised. We feel that though we had no unusual experiences in the wood, others may not have been so fortunate.

MABEL. And be cautious, you dear, what you say to them before they come to.

MRS. COADE. 'Come to'? You puzzle me. And Coady didn't have his muffler.

(Let it be recorded that in their distress for this old lady they forget their own misadventures. PURDIE takes a step toward the curtains in a vague desire to shield her;--and gets a rich reward; he has seen the coming addition to their circle.)

PURDIE (elated and pitiless). It is Matey!

(A butler intrudes who still thinks he is wrapped in fur.)

JOANNA (encouragingly). Do come in.

MATEY. With apologies, ladies and gents . . .  May I ask who is host?

PURDIE (splashing in the temperature that suits him best). A very reasonable request. Third on the left.

MATEY (advancing upon Lob). Merely to ask, sir, if you can direct me to my hotel?

(The sleeper's only response is a alight quiver in one leg.)

The gentleman seems to be reposing.

MRS. COADE. It is Lob.

MATEY. What is lob, ma'am?

MRS. COADE (pleasantly curious). Surely you haven't forgotten?

PURDIE (over-riding her). Anything we can do for you, sir? Just give it a name.

JOANNA (in the same friendly spirit). I hope you are not alone: do say you have some lady friends with you.

MATEY (with an emphasis on his leading word). My wife is with me.

JOANNA. His wife! . . . (With commendation.) You have been quick!

MRS. COADE. I didn't know you were married.

MATEY. Why should you, madam? You talk as if you knew me.

MRS. COADE. Good gracious, do you really think I don't?

PURDIE (indicating delicately that she is subject to a certain softening). Sit down, won't you, my dear sir, and make yourself comfy.

MATEY (accustomed of late to such deferential treatment). Thank you. But my wife . . .

JOANNA (hospitably). Yes, bring her in; we are simply dying to make her acquaintance.

MATEY. You are very good; I am much obliged.

MABEL (as he goes out). Who can she be?

JOANNA (leaping). Who, who, who!

MRS. COADE. But what an extraordinary wood. He doesn't seem to know who he is at all.

MABEL (soothingly). Don't worry about that, Coady darling. He will know soon enough.

JOANNA (again finding the bright side). And so will the little wife! By the way, whoever she is, I hope she is fond of butlers.

MABEL (who has peeped). It is Lady Caroline!   JOANNA (leaping again). Oh, joy, joy! And she was so sure she couldn't take the wrong turning!

(Lady Caroline is evidently still sure of it.)

MATEY. May I present my wife--Lady Caroline Matey.

MABEL (glowing). How do you do!

PURDIE. Your servant, Lady Caroline.

MRS. COADE. Lady Caroline Matey! You?

LADY CAROLINE (without an r in her). Charmed, I'm sure.

JOANNA (neatly). Very pleased to meet any wife of Mr. Matey.

PURDIE (taking the floor). Allow me. The Duchess of Candelabra. The Ladies Helena and Matilda M'Nab. I am the Lord Chancellor.

MABEL. I have wanted so long to make your acquaintance.

LADY CAROLINE. Charmed.

JOANNA (gracefully). These informal meetings are so delightful, don't you think?

LADY CAROLINE. Yes, indeed.

MATEY (the introductions being thus pleasantly concluded). And your friend by the fire?

PURDIE. I will introduce you to him when you wake up--I mean when he wakes up.

MATEY. Perhaps I ought to have said that I am *James* Matey.

LADY CAROLINE (the happy creature). *The* James Matey.

MATEY. A name not, perhaps, unknown in the world of finance.

JOANNA. Finance? Oh, so you did take that clerkship in the City!

MATEY (a little stiffly). I began as a clerk in the City, certainly; and I am not ashamed to admit it.

MRS. COADE (still groping). Fancy that, now. And did it save you?

MATEY. Save me, madam?

JOANNA. Excuse us--we ask odd questions in this house; we only mean, did that keep you honest? Or are you still a pilferer?

LADY CAROLINE (an outraged swan). Husband mine, what does she mean?

JOANNA. No offence; I mean a pilferer on a large scale.

MATEY (remembering certain newspaper jealousy). If you are referring to that Labrador business--or the Working Women's Bank . . .

PURDIE (after the manner of one who has caught a fly). O-ho, got him!

JOANNA (bowing). Yes, those are what I meant.

MATEY (stoutly). There was nothing proved.

JOANNA (like one calling a meeting). Mabel, Jack, here is another of us! You have gone just the same way again, my friend. (Ecstatically.) There is more in it, you see, than taking the wrong turning; you would always take the wrong turning. (The only fitting comment.) Tra-la-la!

LADY CAROLINE. If you are casting any aspersions on my husband, allow me to say that a prouder wife than I does not to-day exist.

MRS. COADE (who finds herself the only clear-headed one). My dear, do be careful.

MABEL. So long as you are satisfied, dear Lady Caroline. But I thought you shrank from all blood that was not blue.

LADY CAROLINE. You thought? Why should you think about me? I beg to assure you that I adore my Jim.

(She seeks his arm, but her Jim has encountered the tray containing coffee cups and a cake, and his hands close on it with a certain intimacy.) Whatever are you doing, Jim?

MATEY. I don't understand it, Caroliny; but somehow I feel at home with this in my hands.

MABEL. 'Caroliny!'

MRS. COADE. Look at me well; don't you remember me?

MATEY (musing). I don't remember you; but I seem to associate you with hard-boiled eggs. (With conviction.) You like your eggs hard-boiled.

PURDIE. Hold on to hard-boiled eggs! She used to tip you especially to see to them.

(MATEY'S hand goes to his pocket.)

Yes, that was the pocket.

LADY CAROLINE (with distaste). Tip!

MATEY (without distaste). Tip!    PURDIE. Jolly word, isn't it?

MATEY (raising the tray). It seems to set me thinking.

LADY CAROLINE (feeling the tap of the hammer). Why is my work-basket in this house?

MRS. COADE. You are living here, you know.

LADY CAROLINE. That is what a person feels. But when did I come? It is very odd, but one feels one ought to say when did one go.

PURDIE. She is coming to with a wush!

MATEY (under the hammer). Mr. . . . Purdie!

LADY CAROLINE. MRS. Coade!

MATEY. The Guv'nor! My clothes!

LADY CAROLINE. One is in evening dress!

JOANNA (charmed to explain). You will understand clearly in a minute, Caroliny. You didn't really take that clerkship, Jim; you went into domestic service; but in the essentials you haven't altered.

PURDIE (pleasantly). I'll have my shaving water at 7.30 sharp, Matey.

MATEY (mechanically). Very good, sir.

LADY CAROLINE. Sir? Midsummer Eve! The wood!

PURDIE. Yes, hold on to the wood.

MATEY. You are . . . you are . . . you are Lady Caroline Laney!

LADY CAROLINE. It is Matey, the butler!

MABEL. You seemed quite happy with him, you know, Lady Caroline.

JOANNA (nicely). We won't tell.

LADY CAROLINE (subsiding). Caroline Matey! And I seemed to like it! How horrible!

MRS. COADE (expressing a general sentiment). It is rather difficult to see what we should do next.

MATEY (tentatively). Perhaps if I were to go downstairs?

PURDIE. It would be conferring a personal favour on us all.

(Thus encouraged MATEY and his tray resume friendly relations with the pantry.)

LADY CAROLINE (with itching fingers as she glares at Lob). It is all that wretch's doing.

(A quiver from Lob's right leg acknowledges the compliment. The gay music of a pipe is heard from outside.)

JOANNA (peeping). Coady!

MRS. COADE. Coady! Why is he so happy?

JOANNA (troubled). Dear, hold my hand.

MRS. COADE (suddenly trembling). Won't he know me?

PURDIE (abashed by that soft face). Mrs. Coade, I 'm sorry. It didn't so much matter about the likes of us, but for your sake I wish Coady hadn't gone out.

MRS. COADE. We that have been happily married this thirty years.

COADE (popping in buoyantly). May I intrude? My name is Coade. The fact is

I was playing about in the wood on a whistle, and I saw your light.

MRS. COADE (the only one with the nerve to answer). Playing about in the wood with a whistle!

COADE (with mild dignity). And why not, madam?

MRS. COADE. Madam! Don't you know me?

COADE. I don't know you . . . (Reflecting.) But I wish I did.

MRS. COADE. Do you? Why?

COADE. If I may say so, you have a very soft, lovable face.

(Several persons breathe again.)

MRS. COADE (inquisitorially). Who was with you, playing whistles in the wood?

(The breathing ceases.)

COADE. No one was with me.

(And is resumed.)

MRS. COADE. No . . . lady?

COADE. Certainly not. (Then he spoils it.) I am a bachelor.

MRS. COADE. A bachelor!

JOANNA. Don't give way, dear; it might be much worse.

MRS. COADE. A bachelor! And you are sure you never spoke to me before? Do think.

COADE. Not to my knowledge. Never . . . except in dreams.

MABEL (taking a risk). What did you say to her in dreams?

COADE. I said, 'My dear.' (This when uttered surprises him.) Odd!

JOANNA. The darling man!

MRS. COADE (wavering). How could you say such things to an old woman?

COADE (thinking it out). Old? I didn't think of you as old. No, no, young-- with the morning dew on your face--coming across a lawn--in a black and green dress--and carrying such a pretty parasol.

MRS. COADE (thrilling). That was how he first met me! He used to love me in black and green; and it *was* a pretty parasol. Look, I am old . . . So it can't be the same woman.

COADE (blinking). Old? Yes, I suppose so. But it is the same soft, lovable face, and the same kind, beaming smile that children could warm their hands at.

MRS. COADE. He always liked my smile.

PURDUE. So do we all.

COADE (to himself). Emma!

MRS. COADE. He hasn't forgotten my name!

COADE. It is sad that we didn't meet long ago. I think I have been waiting for you. I suppose we have met too late? You couldn't overlook my being an old fellow, could you, eh?

JOANNA. How lovely; he is going to propose to her again. Coady, you happy thing, he is wanting the same soft face after thirty years!   MRS. COADE (undoubtedly hopeful). We mustn't be too sure, but I think that is it. (Primly.) What is it exactly that you want, Mr. Coade?

COADE (under a lucky star). I want to have the right to hold the parasol over you. Won't you be my wife, my dear, and so give my long dream of you a happy ending?

MRS. COADE (preening). Kisses are not called for at our age, Coady, but here is a muffler for your old neck.

COADE. My muffler; I have missed it. (It is however to his forehead that his hand goes. Immediately thereafter he misses his sylvan attire.) Why . . . why . . . what . . . who . . . how is this?

PURDIE (nervously). He is coming to.

COADE (reeling and righting himself). Lob!

(The leg indicates that he has got it.)

Bless me, Coady, I went into that wood!

MRS. COADE. And without your muffler, you that are so subject to chills. What are you feeling for in your pocket?

COADE. The whistle. It is a whistle I--Gone! of course it is. It's rather a pity, but . . . (Anxious.) Have I been saying awful things to you?

MABEL. You have been making her so proud. It is a compliment to our whole sex. You had a second chance, and it is her, again!

COADE. Of course it is. (Crestfallen.) But I see I was just the same nice old lazy Coady as before; and I had thought that if I had a second chance, I could do things. I have often said to you, Coady, that it was owing to my being cursed with a competency that I didn't write my great book. But I had no competency this time, and

I haven't written a word.

PURDIE (bitterly enough). That needn't make you feel lonely in this house.

MRS. COADE (in a small voice). You seem to have been quite happy as an old bachelor, dear.

COADE. I am surprised at myself, Emma, but I fear I was.

MRS. COADE (with melancholy perspicacity). I wonder if what it means is that you don't especially need even me. I wonder if it means that you are just the sort of amiable creature that would be happy anywhere, and anyhow?

COADE. Oh dear, can it be as bad as that!

JOANNA (a ministering angel she). Certainly not. It is a romance, and I won't have it looked upon as anything else.

MRS. COADE. Thank you, Joanna. You will try not to miss that whistle, Coady?

COADE (getting the footstool for her). You are all I need.

MRS. COADE. Yes; but I am not so sure as I used to be that it is a great compliment.

JOANNA. Coady, behave.

(There is a knock on the window.)

PURDIE (peeping). Mrs. Dearth! (His spirits revive.) She is alone. Who would have expected that of *her*? MABEL. She is a wild one, Jack, but I sometimes thought rather a dear; I do hope she has got off cheaply.

(ALICE comes to them in her dinner gown.)

PURDIE (the irrepressible). Pleased to see you, stranger.

ALICE (prepared for ejection.) I was afraid such an unceremonious entry might startle you.

PURDIE. Not a bit.

ALICE (defiant). I usually enter a house by the front door.

PURDIE. I have heard that such is the swagger way.

ALICE (simpering). So stupid of me. I lost myself in the wood . . . and . . .

JOANNA (genially). Of course you did. But never mind that; do tell us your name.

LADY CAROLINE (emerging again). Yes, yes, your name.

ALICE. Of course, I am the Honourable Mrs. Finch-Fallowe.

LADY CAROLINE. Of course, of course!

PURDIE. I hope Mr. Finch-Fallowe is very well? We don't know him personally, but may we have the pleasure of seeing him bob up presently?

ALICE. No, I am not sure where he is.

LADY CAROLINE (with point). I wonder if the dear clever police know?

ALICE (imprudently). No, they don't.

(It is a very secondary matter to her. This woman of calamitous fires hears and sees her tormentors chiefly as the probable owner, of the cake which is standing on that tray.) So awkward, I gave my sandwiches to a poor girl and her father whom I met in the wood, and now . . . isn't it a nuisance--I am quite hungry. (So far with a mincing bravado.) May I?

(Without waiting for consent she falls to upon the cake, looking over it like one ready to fight them for it.)

PURDIE (sobered again). Poor soul.

LADY CAROLINE. We are so anxious to know whether you met a friend of ours in the wood--a Mr. Dearth. Perhaps you know him, too?

ALICE. Dearth? I don't know any Dearth.

MRS. COADE. Oh, dear what a wood!

LADY CAROLINE. He is quite a front door sort of man; knocks and rings, you know.

PURDIE. Don't worry her.

ALICE (gnawing). I meet so many; you see I go out a great deal. I have visiting-cards--printed ones.

LADY CAROLINE. How very distingue. Perhaps Mr. Dearth has painted your portrait; he is an artist.

ALICE. Very likely; they all want to paint me. I daresay that is the man to whom I gave my sandwiches.

MRS. COADE. But I thought you said he had a daughter?

ALICE. Such a pretty girl; I gave her half a crown.

COADE. A daughter? That can't be Dearth.

PURDIE (darkly). Don't be too sure. Was the man you speak of a rather chop-fallen, gone-to-seed sort of person.

ALICE. No, I thought him such a jolly, attractive man.

COADE. Dearth jolly, attractive! Oh no. Did he say anything about his wife?

LADY CAROLINE, Yes, do try to remember if he mentioned her.

ALICE (snapping). No, he didn't.

PURDIE. He was far from jolly in her time.

ALICE (with an archness for which the cake is responsible). Perhaps that was the lady's fault.

(The last of the adventurers draws nigh, carolling a French song as he comes.)

COADE. Dearth's voice. He sounds quite merry!

JOANNA (protecting). Alice, you poor thing.

PURDIE. This is going to be horrible.

(A clear-eyed man of lusty gait comes in.)

DEARTH. I am sorry to bounce in on you in this way, but really I have an excuse. I am a painter of sorts, and . . .

(He sees he has brought some strange discomfort here.)

MRS. COADE. I must say, Mr. Dearth, I am delighted to see you looking so well. Like a new man, isn't he?

(No one dares to answer.)

DEARTH. I am certainly very well, if you care to know. But did I tell you my name?

JOANNA (for some one has to speak). No, but--but we have an instinct in this house.

DEARTH. Well, it doesn't matter. Here is the situation; my daughter and I have just met in the wood a poor woman famishing for want of food. We were as happy as grigs ourselves, and the sight of her distress rather cut us up. Can you give me something for her? Why are you looking so startled? (Seeing the remains of the cake.) May I have this?

(A shrinking movement from one of them draws his attention, and he recognises in her the woman of whom he has been speaking. He sees her in fine clothing and he grows stern.)

I feel I can't be mistaken; it was you I met in the wood? Have you been playing some trick on me? (To the others.) It was for her I wanted the food.

ALICE (her hand guarding the place where his gift lies). Have you come to take back the money you gave me?

DEARTH. Your dress! You were almost in rags when I saw you outside.

ALICE (frightened as she discovers how she is now attired). I don't . . . understand . . .

COADE (gravely enough). For that matter, Dearth, I daresay you were different in the wood, too.

(DEARTH sees his own clothing.)

DEARTH. What . . . !

ALICE (frightened). Where am I? (To Mrs. Coade.) I seem to know you . . . do I?

MRS. COADE (motherly). Yes, you do; hold my hand, and you will soon remember all about it.

JOANNA. I am afraid, Mr. Dearth, it is harder for you than for the rest of us.

PURDIE (looking away). I wish I could help you, but I can't; I am a rotter.

MABEL. We are awfully sorry. Don't you remember . . . Midsummer Eve?

DEARTH (controlling himself). Midsummer Eve? This room. Yes, this room . . . You was it you? . . . were going out to look for something . . . The tree of knowledge, wasn't it? Somebody wanted me to go, too . . .  Who was that? A lady, I think . . . Why did she ask me to go? What was I doing here? I was smoking a cigar . . . I laid it down, there . . . (He finds the cigar.) Who was the lady?

ALICE (feebly). Something about a second chance.

MRS. COADE. Yes, you poor dear, you thought you could make so much of it.

DEARTH. A lady who didn't like me-- (With conviction.) She had good reasons, too--but what were they . . . ?

ALICE. A little old man! He did it. What did he do?

(The hammer is raised.)

DEARTH. I am . . . it is coming back--I am not the man I thought myself.

ALICE. I am not Mrs. Finch-Fallowe. Who am I?

DEARTH (staring at her). You were that lady.

ALICE. It is you--my husband!

(She is overcome.)

MRS. COADE. My dear, you are much better off, so far as I can see, than if you were Mrs. Finch-Fallowe.

ALICE (with passionate knowledge). Yes, yes indeed! (Generously.) But he isn't.

DEARTH. Alice! . . . I--(He tries to smile.) I didn't know you when I was in the wood with Margaret. She . . . she . . . Margaret . . . (The hammer falls.)

O my God!

(He buries his face in his hands.)

ALICE. I wish--I wish--

(She presses his shoulder fiercely and then stalks out by the door.)

PURDIE (to LOB, after a time). You old ruffian.

DEARTH. No, I am rather fond of him, our lonely, friendly little host. Lob, I thank thee for that hour.

(The seedy-looking fellow passes from the scene.)

COADE. Did you see that his hand is shaking again?

PURDIE. The watery eye has come back.

JOANNA. And yet they are both quite nice people.

PURDIE (finding the tragedy of it). We are all quite nice people.

MABEL. If she were not such a savage!

PURDIE. I daresay there is nothing the matter with her except that she would always choose the wrong man, good man or bad man, but the wrong man for her.

COADE. We can't change.

MABEL. Jack says the brave ones can.

JOANNA. 'The ones with the thin bright faces.'

MABEL. Then there is hope for you and me, Jack.

PURDIE (ignobly). I don't expect so.

JOANNA (wandering about the room, like one renewing acquaintance with it after returning from a journey). Hadn't we better go to bed? It must be getting late.

PURDIE. Hold on to bed! (They all brighten.)

MATEY (entering). Breakfast is quite ready.

(They exclaim.)

LADY CAROLINE. My watch has stopped.

JOANNA. And mine. Just as well perhaps!

MABEL. There is a smell of coffee.

(The gloom continues to lift.)

COADE. Come along, Coady; I do hope you have not been tiring your foot.

MRS. COADE. I shall give it a good rest to-morrow, dear.

MATEY. I have given your egg six minutes, ma'am.

(They set forth once more upon the eternal round. The curious JOANNA remains behind.)

JOANNA. A strange experiment, Matey; does it ever have any permanent effect?

MATEY (on whom it has had none). So far as I know, not often, miss; but, I believe, once in a while.

(There is hope in this for the brave ones. If we could wait long enough we might see the DEARTHS breasting their way into the light.)

*He* could tell you.

(The elusive person thus referred to kicks responsively, meaning perhaps that none of the others will change till there is a tap from another hammer. But when MATEY goes to rout him from his chair he is no longer there. His disappearance is no shock to MATEY, who shrugs his shoulders and opens the windows to let in the glory of a summer morning. The garden has returned, and our queer little hero is busy at work among his flowers. A lark is rising.)

# The End

www.bookjungle.com *email: sales@bookjungle.com fax: 630-214-0564 mail: Book Jungle PO Box 2226 Champaign, IL 61825*

### The Codes Of Hammurabi And Moses
### W. W. Davies

QTY

The discovery of the Hammurabi Code is one of the greatest achievements of archaeology, and is of paramount interest, not only to the student of the Bible, but also to all those interested in ancient history...

**Religion**     **ISBN:** *1-59462-338-4*     **Pages:132**
*MSRP $12.95*

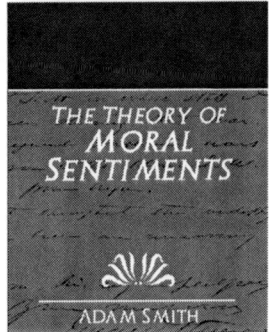

### The Theory of Moral Sentiments
### Adam Smith

QTY

This work from 1749 contains original theories of conscience amd moral judgment and it is the foundation for systemof morals.

**Philosophy**   **ISBN:** *1-59462-777-0*     **Pages:536**
*MSRP $19.95*

### Jessica's First Prayer
### Hesba Stretton

QTY

In a screened and secluded corner of one of the many railway-bridges which span the streets of London there could be seen a few years ago, from five o'clock every morning until half past eight, a tidlly set-out coffee-stall, consisting of a trestle and board, upon which stood two large tin cans, with a small fire of charcoal burning under each so as to keep the coffee boiling during the early hours of the morning when the work-people were thronging into the city on their way to their daily toil...

**Pages:84**

**Childrens**    **ISBN:** *1-59462-373-2*     *MSRP $9.95*

### My Life and Work
### Henry Ford

QTY

Henry Ford revolutionized the world with his implementation of mass production for the Model T automobile. Gain valuable business insight into his life and work with his own auto-biography... "We have only started on our development of our country we have not as yet, with all our talk of wonderful progress, done more than scratch the surface. The progress has been wonderful enough but..."

**Pages:300**

**Biographies/**   **ISBN:** *1-59462-198-5*     *MSRP $21.95*

## The Art of Cross-Examination
## Francis Wellman

QTY

I presume it is the experience of every author, after his first book is published upon an important subject, to be almost overwhelmed with a wealth of ideas and illustrations which could readily have been included in his book, and which to his own mind, at least, seem to make a second edition inevitable. Such certainly was the case with me; and when the first edition had reached its sixth impression in five months, I rejoiced to learn that it seemed to my publishers that the book had met with a sufficiently favorable reception to justify a second and considerably enlarged edition. ...

Reference     ISBN: *1-59462-647-2*

**Pages:412**

*MSRP $19.95*

## On the Duty of Civil Disobedience
## Henry David Thoreau

QTY

Thoreau wrote his famous essay, On the Duty of Civil Disobedience, as a protest against an unjust but popular war and the immoral but popular institution of slave-owning. He did more than write—he declined to pay his taxes, and was hauled off to gaol in consequence. Who can say how much this refusal of his hastened the end of the war and of slavery ?

Law          ISBN: *1-59462-747-9*

**Pages:48**

*MSRP $7.45*

## Dream Psychology Psychoanalysis for Beginners
## Sigmund Freud

QTY

Sigmund Freud, born Sigismund Schlomo Freud (May 6, 1856 - September 23, 1939), was a Jewish-Austrian neurologist and psychiatrist who co-founded the psychoanalytic school of psychology. Freud is best known for his theories of the unconscious mind, especially involving the mechanism of repression; his redefinition of sexual desire as mobile and directed towards a wide variety of objects; and his therapeutic techniques, especially his understanding of transference in the therapeutic relationship and the presumed value of dreams as sources of insight into unconscious desires.

Psychology    ISBN: *1-59462-905-6*

**Pages:196**

*MSRP $15.45*

## The Miracle of Right Thought
## Orison Swett Marden

QTY

Believe with all of your heart that you will do what you were made to do. When the mind has once formed the habit of holding cheerful, happy, prosperous pictures, it will not be easy to form the opposite habit. It does not matter how improbable or how far away this realization may see, or how dark the prospects may be, if we visualize them as best we can, as vividly as possible, hold tenaciously to them and vigorously struggle to attain them, they will gradually become actualized, realized in the life. But a desire, a longing without endeavor, a yearning abandoned or held indifferently will vanish without realization.

Self Help     ISBN: *1-59462-644-8*

**Pages:360**

*MSRP $25.45*

www.**bookjungle**.com *email: sales@bookjungle.com fax: 630-214-0564 mail: Book Jungle PO Box 2226 Champaign, IL 61825*

QTY

**The Rosicrucian Cosmo-Conception Mystic Christianity** *by Max Heindel* ISBN: *1-59462-188-8* **$38.95**
*The Rosicrucian Cosmo-conception is not dogmatic, neither does it appeal to any other authority than the reason of the student. It is: not controversial, but is: sent forth in the, hope that it may help to clear..* New Age/Religion Pages 646

**Abandonment To Divine Providence** *by Jean-Pierre de Caussade* ISBN: *1-59462-228-0* **$25.95**
*"The Rev. Jean Pierre de Caussade was one of the most remarkable spiritual writers of the Society of Jesus in France in the 18th Century. His death took place at Toulouse in 1751. His works have gone through many editions and have been republished...* Inspirational/Religion Pages 400

**Mental Chemistry** *by Charles Haanel* ISBN: *1-59462-192-6* **$23.95**
*Mental Chemistry allows the change of material conditions by combining and appropriately utilizing the power of the mind. Much like applied chemistry creates something new and unique out of careful combinations of chemicals the mastery of mental chemistry...* New Age Pages 354

**The Letters of Robert Browning and Elizabeth Barret Barrett 1845-1846 vol II** ISBN: *1-59462-193-4* **$35.95**
*by Robert Browning and Elizabeth Barrett* Biographies Pages 596

**Gleanings In Genesis (volume I)** *by Arthur W. Pink* ISBN: *1-59462-130-6* **$27.45**
*Appropriately has Genesis been termed "the seed plot of the Bible" for in it we have, in germ form, almost all of the great doctrines which are afterwards fully developed in the books of Scripture which follow...* Religion/Inspirational Pages 420

**The Master Key** *by L. W. de Laurence* ISBN: *1-59462-001-6* **$30.95**
*In no branch of human knowledge has there been a more lively increase of the spirit of research during the past few years than in the study of Psychology, Concentration and Mental Discipline. The requests for authentic lessons in Thought Control, Mental Discipline and...* New Age/Business Pages 422

**The Lesser Key Of Solomon Goetia** *by L. W. de Laurence* ISBN: *1-59462-092-X* **$9.95**
*This translation of the first book of the "Lernegton" which is now for the first time made accessible to students of Talismanic Magic was done, after careful collation and edition, from numerous Ancient Manuscripts in Hebrew, Latin, and French...* New Age/Occult Pages 92

**Rubaiyat Of Omar Khayyam** *by Edward Fitzgerald* ISBN: *1-59462-332-5* **$13.95**
*Edward Fitzgerald, whom the world has already learned, in spite of his own efforts to remain within the shadow of anonymity, to look upon as one of the rarest poets of the century, was born at Bredfield, in Suffolk, on the 31st of March, 1809. He was the third son of John Purcell...* Music Pages 172

**Ancient Law** *by Henry Maine* ISBN: *1-59462-128-4* **$29.95**
*The chief object of the following pages is to indicate some of the earliest ideas of mankind, as they are reflected in Ancient Law, and to point out the relation of those ideas to modern thought.* Religion/History Pages 452

**Far-Away Stories** *by William J. Locke* ISBN: *1-59462-129-2* **$19.45**
*"Good wine needs no bush, but a collection of mixed vintages does. And this book is just such a collection. Some of the stories I do not want to remain buried for ever in the museum files of dead magazine-numbers an author's not unpardonable vanity..."* Fiction Pages 272

**Life of David Crockett** *by David Crockett* ISBN: *1-59462-250-7* **$27.45**
*"Colonel David Crockett was one of the most remarkable men of the times in which he lived. Born in humble life, but gifted with a strong will, an indomitable courage, and unremitting perseverance...* Biographies/New Age Pages 424

**Lip-Reading** *by Edward Nitchie* ISBN: *1-59462-206-X* **$25.95**
*Edward B. Nitchie, founder of the New York School for the Hard of Hearing, now the Nitchie School of Lip-Reading, Inc, wrote "LIP-READING Principles and Practice". The development and perfecting of this meritorious work on lip-reading was an undertaking...* How-to Pages 400

**A Handbook of Suggestive Therapeutics, Applied Hypnotism, Psychic Science** ISBN: *1-59462-214-0* **$24.95**
*by Henry Munro* Health New Age/Health Self-help Pages 376

**A Doll's House: and Two Other Plays** *by Henrik Ibsen* ISBN: *1-59462-112-8* **$19.95**
*Henrik Ibsen created this classic when in revolutionary 1848 Rome. Introducing some striking concepts in playwriting for the realist genre, this play has been studied the world over.* Fiction/Classics/Plays 308

**The Light of Asia** *by sir Edwin Arnold* ISBN: *1-59462-204-3* **$13.95**
*In this poetic masterpiece, Edwin Arnold describes the life and teachings of Buddha. The man who was to become known as Buddha to the world was born as Prince Gautama of India but he rejected the worldly riches and abandoned the reigns of power when...* Religion/History/Biographies Pages 170

**The Complete Works of Guy de Maupassant** *by Guy de Maupassant* ISBN: *1-59462-157-8* **$16.95**
*"For days and days, nights and nights, I had dreamed of that first kiss which was to consecrate our engagement, and I knew not on what spot I should put my lips..."* Fiction/Classics Pages 240

**The Art of Cross-Examination** *by Francis L. Wellman* ISBN: *1-59462-309-0* **$26.95**
*Written by a renowned trial lawyer, Wellman imparts his experience and uses case studies to explain how to use psychology to extract desired information through questioning.* How-to/Science/Reference Pages 408

**Answered or Unanswered?** *by Louisa Vaughan* ISBN: *1-59462-248-5* **$10.95**
*Miracles of Faith in China* Religion Pages 112

**The Edinburgh Lectures on Mental Science (1909)** *by Thomas* ISBN: *1-59462-008-3* **$11.95**
*This book contains the substance of a course of lectures recently given by the writer in the Queen Street Hall, Edinburgh. Its purpose is to indicate the Natural Principles governing the relation between Mental Action and Material Conditions...* New Age Psychology Pages 148

**Ayesha** *by H. Rider Haggard* ISBN: *1-59462-301-5* **$24.95**
*Verily and indeed it is the unexpected that happens! Probably if there was one person upon the earth from whom the Editor of this, and of a certain previous history, did not expect to hear again...* Classics Pages 380

**Ayala's Angel** *by Anthony Trollope* ISBN: *1-59462-352-X* **$29.95**
*The two girls were both pretty; but Lucy who was twenty-one who supposed to be simple and comparatively unattractive, whereas Ayala was credited, as her Bombwhat romantic name might show, with poetic charm and a taste for romance. Ayala when her father died was nineteen...* Fiction Pages 484

**The American Commonwealth** *by James Bryce* ISBN: *1-59462-286-8* **$34.45**
*An interpretation of American democratic political theory. It examines political mechanics and society from the perspective of Scotsman James Bryce* Politics Pages 572

**Stories of the Pilgrims** *by Margaret P. Pumphrey* ISBN: *1-59462-116-0* **$17.95**
*This book explores pilgrims religious oppression in England as well as their escape to Holland and eventual crossing to America on the Mayflower, and their early days in New England...* History Pages 268

**QTY**

**The Fasting Cure** *by Sinclair Upton*                                    ISBN: *1-59462-222-1*  **$13.95**
*In the Cosmopolitan Magazine for May, 1910, and in the Contemporary Review (London) for April, 1910, I published an article dealing with my experiences in fasting. I have written a great many magazine articles, but never one which attracted so much attention... New Age/Self Help/Health Pages 164*

**Hebrew Astrology** *by Sepharial*                                    ISBN: *1-59462-308-2*  **$13.45**
*In these days of advanced thinking it is a matter of common observation that we have left many of the old landmarks behind and that we are now pressing forward to greater heights and to a wider horizon than that which represented the mind-content of our progenitors... Astrology Pages 144*

**Thought Vibration or The Law of Attraction in the Thought World**    ISBN: *1-59462-127-6*  **$12.95**
*by William Walker Atkinson*                                              *Psychology/Religion Pages 144*

**Optimism** *by Helen Keller*                                        ISBN: *1-59462-108-X*  **$15.95**
*Helen Keller was blind, deaf, and mute since 19 months old, yet famously learned how to overcome these handicaps, communicate with the world, and spread her lectures promoting optimism.  An inspiring read for everyone... Biographies/Inspirational Pages 84*

**Sara Crewe** *by Frances Burnett*                                    ISBN: *1-59462-360-0*  **$9.45**
*In the first place, Miss Minchin lived in London. Her home was a large, dull, tall one, in a large, dull square, where all the houses were alike, and all the sparrows were alike, and where all the door-knockers made the same heavy sound... Childrens/Classic Pages 88*

**The Autobiography of Benjamin Franklin** *by Benjamin Franklin*      ISBN: *1-59462-135-7*  **$24.95**
*The Autobiography of Benjamin Franklin has probably been more extensively read than any other American historical work, and no other book of its kind has had such ups and downs of fortune. Franklin lived for many years in England, where he was agent... Biographies/History Pages 332*

| | |
|---|---|
| **Name** | |
| **Email** | |
| **Telephone** | |
| **Address** | |
| | |
| **City, State ZIP** | |

☐ **Credit Card**        ☐ **Check / Money Order**

| | |
|---|---|
| **Credit Card Number** | |
| **Expiration Date** | |
| **Signature** | |

*Please Mail to:   Book Jungle*
*PO Box 2226*
*Champaign, IL 61825*
*or Fax to:        630-214-0564*

## ORDERING INFORMATION
**web**: *www.bookjungle.com*
**email**: *sales@bookjungle.com*
**fax**: *630-214-0564*
**mail**: *Book Jungle  PO Box 2226  Champaign, IL 61825*
**or PayPal** *to sales@bookjungle.com*

*Please contact us for bulk discounts*

## DIRECT-ORDER TERMS

**20% Discount if You Order
Two or More Books**
Free Domestic Shipping!
Accepted: Master Card, Visa,
Discover, American Express

Lightning Source UK Ltd.
Milton Keynes UK
14 October 2009

144905UK00001B/28/P